What people are saying about . . .

HI GOD, ONE MORE THING

"Nicole Crank knows regular, daily conversations with God are essential to our Christian walk, especially during life's most challenging moments. *Hi God, One More Thing* gives voice to those times when we need God the most but can't find the words. With heartfelt insight and truth from God's Word, this devotional will inspire you again and again!"

Chris Hodges, Senior Pastor, Church of the Highlands, Author of "The Daniel Dilemma" and "What's Next?"

"So many people struggle with how to talk to God. Understandably so! Sometimes, we feel as if our problems are too insignificant to even mention to the Creator of the Universe. God desires a relationship with us, and all relationships start with a conversation. In her book, *Hi God, One More Thing,* Nicole Crank demonstrates how our prayers can be conversational, honest, and even simple. If you struggle with how to talk to God, let this book help you start with, 'Hi God.'"

Craig Groeschel, Pastor of Life.Church and New York Times Best Selling Author

"Worship First: an awesome reminder to give God your best, FIRST! I'm So Embarrassed. When the world gets a hold of a private matter you feel yucky and you almost cave into it, believing that's your new identity. This devotion is a huge encouragement that God does not see you through the lens of your past, or your mistakes."

Michelle Williams of Destiny's Child, Actress, Speaker, Contestant on "The Masked Singer"

"Nicole Crank has done it, yet again! Her first *Hi God* book was a game-changer! And now this one, *Hi God, One More Thing*, is the icing on the cake! This book does the work for you. When the enemy tries to mute you with despair, heartbreak, and fear, this book gives you your *Popeye's spinach*, called the Word, to move those mountains. Brilliant! Love it! Great job!"

Real Talk Kim, Television& Radio Personality, Best-selling author, Co-pastor Limitless Church, Fayetteville, GA

"I know my friend Nicole Crank is such a believer in the power of prayer that she would read my Gigi books to her daughter to show her how to talk to God, even as a little child. With that same heart, Nicole tries to connect the inner child in all of us to our father and Creator, no matter our physical age or our spiritual age, trying to make tough conversations easy."

Sheila Walsh, Author of "Praying Women"

"Our God can handle the tough stuff! Pastor Nicole makes jumping into the depths of authentic and raw prayer accessible to anyone. *Hi God, One More Thing* will fire you up! I believe you will encounter our great and good God in a more intimate and powerful way!"

Amy Groeschel, Author, Founder of Branch 15,
Leader of Women's Ministry & Co-founder Life.Church

"I am a warrior—a servant of God—a world changer—an inspiration—a living testimony of God's glory! From a place of Victory, I push past all challenges I may face, armed with weapons to dominate any battle I may encounter. This book, *Hi God, One More Thing* and the one before by Pastor Crank, has supplied me with an intimate road map to the conversations others are afraid to have with believers. I can go to any chapter and relate, getting understanding, clarity, and confirmation from the Word of God to strengthen me, giving me peace and power over any circumstance. Pastor has unleashed a book that is intimate and powerful, giving me immediate solutions to any situation, and keeping me focused on the promise God has made to me!!! I encourage you to grab one! Stay armed with it, keep it easy to access, and remain Victorious!"

Laurieann Gibson, Producer, Director, Choreographer,
Artist, Judge—"So You Think You Can Dance,"
Choreographer—MTV "Making the Band"

"Sometimes, finding the words to express our feelings and just talk to God about them can be difficult. In her book, *Hi God, One More Thing*, Nicole Crank manages to do just that. Whether it is about feeling overwhelmed, or afraid, or confused, or alone, or angry; in this book you will find the words to pray. Each section is a quick read, thus making talking with God seem easy! You will enjoy this book!"

Holly Wagner, Founding Pastor Oasis Church,
Founder "She Rises," Author "Find Your Brave"

"This book speaks to your mind, body, and soul! It's real honest and practical, in so many ways, to help you overcome everyday life situations. We all face pressure. We all feel overwhelmed by life's challenges. It's important that we stop and talk to God and give Him our cares. We can't go through life alone! We need to stop and talk to God who knows what we're facing and has the answers we need to defeat the enemy!"

Kandy and Ron Isley—The Isley Brothers

"I just love the excitement that comes with trying something new. It's exhilarating! The enemy has tried to stop us from experiencing the joy of trying new things, on our journey with God, by throwing negative thoughts at us that cause anxiety and allow fear of the unknown to set in. We become afraid because we feel as if we have to do all the driving. But, as Nicole mentions, *'All I have to do is HOLD ON, I do not have to drive.'* Now I don't know about you, but I thoroughly enjoy being driven and being able to fully experience all the sights from the passenger side of the car. Once we understand that all we have to do is allow God to lead us, we can truly experience His best. Which is the reason Jesus came, so that we can abundantly enjoy life. As I continue in my journey with God, He's taking me places I've never imagined for myself, meeting people I've admired from afar, and doing things that can only be done with Him right beside me. Was I afraid? Yes! Was I nervous? Absolutely! But I would not trade one second of the ride God has taken me on because, in the end, the fruit of it, the lives of His people being changed, renewed, and restored has all been worth it. This book has shown me that there is even more out there to experience, with Gods help. I highly recommend this book to anyone, but especially those who have had challenges with truly trusting God and letting go. Nicole's book will help you go further with God and enjoy the good life He intended for you. Nicole takes you on a journey to take a bold step of faith, step into the car, put your seatbelt on, relax in His presence, and enjoy the ride with God!"

Dr. DeeDee Freeman, Author, Founder "Women Walking in The Word", Wife to Pastor Mike Freeman, Spirit of Faith Christian Center.

HI GOD,

ONE MORE THING

HI GOD,
ONE
MORE
THING

HOW TO TALK TO GOD ABOUT
THE *TOUGH STUFF*

NICOLE CRANK

Published by:

Four Rivers Media Group
225 W. Seminole Blvd.
Suite #105
Sanford, Florida. 32771

Hardback ISBN: 978-1-950718-32-0

Printed in the United States of America

First Edition

To my precious and loving husband, David
—who had to listen to my complaining to him
when I should have been talking to God.
I'm learning, honey.

TABLE OF CONTENTS

INTRODUCTION

I don't know that I've met you before, so it might seem weird to just jump right into familiar conversation; but this is too good for you to miss. And get used to this familiar conversation thing, because this book is full of it—including all the CAPS and *italics* they wanted to edit out. I fought to keep them in because this isn't a book (even though it kinda feels like one as you turn the physical pages). This is a conversation.

You guys (my *Hi God, It's Me Again* friends) have been seriously hounding me EVERY SINGLE DAY to write another Hi God book with more topics. So we've been hard at work. I say 'we' because I'm writing it, but it also takes editors, proofers, graphics design, layout, a printer, a publisher, and all the things.

This book is about to be printed, and we realized there wasn't an introduction. They want one TODAY. Today? Um, God? I'm not feeling inspired. I don't know what to say. It immediately starts to dawn on me that THIS is exactly WHY I wrote the book in the first place! We feel like we don't know what to say, especially to someone who's as big of a deal as God is.

I dodge and deflect to go into my personal study time—reading. That seems easier.

It was a cloudy day and a little dark at seven in the morning as I sat down to write this introduction. But then, I saw the sun pop out. Well, that's not exactly true. I saw the sun shine onto a chair near the one I was sitting in. I leaned up and looked outside…and saw the most majestic view of the sun coming through the clouds, in this royally golden sort of way, and reflect off the water right through my window. I hadn't been able to see the view from where I'd been curled up. I sat back again to return to reading, and missed the splendor.

Why?

Why would I sit back and miss getting to see it?

Am I too lazy?

Too habitual?

Am I scared of one more sit up?

Did it seem like just "too much energy" to move?

Did it make me feel "extra"?

I quit asking questions, and did something different: I sat in a different seat. I did have to leave what I'd been doing to do a new thing. But it turns out that I chose a much better thing. I could now see the view. I could feel the sun. I could see the majesty of God shining through the clouds. This wasn't just a glimpse followed by a return to the old grind. Now, I did what I did in the full unadulterated shine of the son . . . I mean sun.

Such improvement is so close; and yet, I almost missed it.

That's why I'm glad you're here. I feel that many of you have been SO CLOSE to breakthrough. You've been saying those words to God; forgiving those turkeys—ahem, people—who have wronged you; leaning in a little more. And I truly believe *Hi God, One More Thing* will do more than get you to "lean in"—I believe it will prompt you to finally change seats—to get a spiritual "seat upgrade."

If you've been seeing others bask in the light and have wanted some of your own, I am convinced that reading this book OUT LOUD (yup, there are those pesky caps again, AND I made a funny face when I said those words in my head) . . . let me say it again: OUT LOUD, will help you go from seeing the light to living in it.

You're about to get to know God better, and begin trusting him with even more intimate and guarded parts of you. The amazing thing is, he never disappoints. He is not only going to meet you in this new space—he is going to exceed your expectations.

You don't necessarily need to read this book "in order." Read the Table of Contents. Find the chapter that speaks to you in your present moment. And have that talk with God today. Oh, but don't leave me out! When you do, hit me up on social media or my website (nicolecrank.com), and tell me about what he said. I can't wait to hear the revelations, direction, healing, and wisdom he gives you.

I'm going to stop talking now, so you can talk to him.

I DON'T HAVE TIME

Hi God. *Tick tock* goes the clock. I've really been hustling today. I mean, I'm giving it my best! I just glanced up at the clock and it's almost dinnertime. HOW?

I still have SO MUCH I have to do today. I haven't even gotten to my morning prayer time, working out, or the laundry!

How is it that I mean to get up and put you first, yet somehow, you get squeezed between "Oh no, I have to fix that!" and "What in the world just happened?" That's *if* I get to talk to you at all! It's been a lot more like I'm trying to fit you in . . . like I'm closing the door really fast. It's more like just a few minutes with you to get through the day than a real meeting with the God of Heaven and Earth!

I want you in my life! I mean . . .I really NEED you to tell me what to do. I have NO IDEA how to figure life out. I've got to have time with you so you can give me some clarity. I desperately want to be "in tune" with my purpose. And that doesn't work when I'm rushing in for some quick time with you because life has so many demands.

I have to reframe my thinking about this TIME thing! I have to get my priorities right! If I let time dictate my life, I'll never fulfill my calling. Time is the master that will do its best to never allow me to win. I'm turning Airplane Mode "on" so that I don't get distracted and miss out on time with you.

Time with you, God, isn't time lost. Time with you is SOWING. It gives me a chance to reap the benefits of MORE time. When I get with you, God, the pressures and responsibilities of life seem to fade away.

I get wiser, faster, stronger, and more able. I stop wasting time, and I dodge bad decisions because I'm leaning on the One who can keep me from turning down the wrong road.

Being with you doesn't cost me time, because you REDEEM the time. I trade my heartaches and hurts for grace and mercy. I will spend time with you because you are the multiplier of time! I have TIME for TIME with you!

You do not operate on a timetable. You operate on eternity! Time is of no consequence to you!

God's Word

"But as for me, I watch in hope for the Lord,
I wait for God my Savior; my God will hear me."
—Micah 7:7 NIV

"Better is one day in your courts than a thousand
elsewhere; I would rather be a doorkeeper in the
house of my God than dwell in the tents of the
wicked."
—Psalm 84:10 NIV

"See then that you walk circumspectly,
not as fools but as wise, redeeming the time,
because the days are evil. Therefore do not
be unwise, but understand what the will
of the Lord is."
—Ephesians 5:15-17 NKJV

WHEN I FEEL WEAK

Hi God. I'm laying here trying to get up. But, I don't think I have the strength. I feel like I just can't do *one more* conversation about the *same* thing—one more lap around the mountain, one more day like yesterday. It seems like I keep trying with every ounce of what I have to give, and yet . . .

I feel weak. At least in my own strength. But you didn't ask me to make this journey alone. You've always been there, wanting me to lean on you. Without weakness, I might start to think I don't need you. The exact opposite is true! I can't do it without you!

You use my weakness as an indicator to let me know that it's time to lean on you. It's time to get out of my own head and get into the eyes of Spirit and faith that you know best. You will never leave me! It's time to walk by faith. I can't do it alone. I wasn't manufactured that way. I was designed to do *with* you!

My humility allows my weakness to be apparent.

When I'm weak, you're strong! It's my moment to realize that I was not created to live independently and gallop through life on my own. I was formed, manufactured, and wired from the factory to be dependent on the operating system of Heaven.

When the Israelites stared at the walls of Jericho, marching around it for six days in a row . . . and nothing happened; not a thing had changed and there was no sign of it *ever* changing . . .but God!

You are my strength! You fill in my gaps. You're everything that I'm not. And you never fail me. You never leave me. You never leave me hanging out to dry. You cover me when I'm exposed. You protect me when I don't even know there's an enemy trying to attack. You catch me when I fall and set me on my feet again.

When I am weak and humbly submit to you, you come out strong. Move, Lord!

"For we do not have a high priest who is unable to sympathize with our weaknesses, but one who in every respect has been tempted as we are, yet without sin."
—Hebrews 4:15 ESV

"The Lord himself goes before you and will be with you; he will never leave you nor forsake you. Do not be afraid; do not be discouraged."
—Deuteronomy 31:8 NIV

"Likewise the Spirit helps us in our weakness. For we do not know what to pray for as we ought, but the Spirit himself intercedes for us with groanings too deep for words."
—Romans 8:26 ESV

"So on the second day they marched around the city once and returned to the camp. They did this for six days. On the seventh day, they got up at daybreak and marched around the city seven times in the same manner, except that on that day they circled the city seven times."
—Joshua 6:14-15 NIV

TIED DOWN

Hi God. I feel so . . . restricted—so tied down. It seems like the weight of the world is on my shoulders. As soon as I try to offload part of this mess to somebody else, another round of craziness pops up, they drop the ball, or something crashes. Sometimes, it just seems easier to do it all myself.

That is, until I'm living on coffee and no sleep. That's when everybody starts to tell me that I'm grouchy. I don't think this strategy has me winning any popularity contests! I tell them I'm fine; but I know I'm not. This stress . . .this confusion . . .this burnout pace . . .this can't be your best for me.

You said to take your yoke upon me, and that I would find rest. I want to do that—I really do! It's just that I don't think I can carry a single feather more than the junk I have on my shoulders at the moment.

But you're not trying to add anything. You're looking for a trade. You want my yoke. And then, I get yours. But what exactly *is* your yoke?

Your yoke is trusting you with all the situations I think *I* have to fix.

Your yoke is giving grace to those people that I'd really rather slander and tear down.

Your yoke is patience with the slow things in life: the slow traffic, the slow response, the slow line, and the slow customer service.

Your yoke is humility: giving others the chance to get it right. After all, I need that chance in so many areas of my own life.

Your yoke is compassion: actually allowing myself to feel for other people instead of just myself.

Your yoke is loving the unlovely. I've been forcing everyone to deal with *my* crap; it's time I return the favor.

Your yoke is following you instead of stepping out and expecting you to meet me wherever I decide to go.

Your yoke is asking instead of telling.

Your yoke is releasing my junk, my control, my burden, my fear, and all the weight of the questions I think I have to answer by myself. It's putting down every single thing I think I have to do, and simply taking up your yoke.

You've promised to carry this . . .but you won't do it until I release it to you.

In return, you will give me love, compassion, grace, patience, humility, and trust. These are the things I get to carry while you strap on my heartache, stress, confusion, frustration, blind-sided shock, and bewilderment.

This is an amazing trade! I can't believe I haven't taken you up on this before now. Today, Father God, I take on your yoke and I leave mine to you.

God's Word

"Come to Me, all you who labor and are
heavy laden, and I will give you rest.
Take My yoke upon you and learn from Me,
for I am gentle and lowly in heart,
and you will find rest for your souls."
—Matthew 11:28-29 NKJV

"Don't worry about anything.
No matter what happens, tell God about everything.
Ask and pray, and give thanks to him."
—Philippians 4:6 NIRV

"Be humble in the presence of God's mighty
power, and he will honor you when the
time comes. God cares for you,
so turn all your worries over to him."
—1 Peter 5:6-7 CEV

I CAN'T FIX IT

Hi God. I'm looking at something right now that I don't even know how to handle. I can't fix it. I can't make it go away. I can't repair it. And I feel helpless, weak, and vulnerable!

Weak . . .When I am weak, your strength shows through. I don't get to the beginning of you until I reach the end of me. If I could make it all better, I would; but then I wouldn't need you. I probably wouldn't even get you involved. I'd just march right ahead in foolish pride, making decisions without even consulting you, because "I've got it." Famous last words.

The things I can't fix are the things I was never meant to fix. I was created to rely on you for every decision, every need, and every desire. You're my Provider—for every single thing I need. Whether I need you to shut the mouth of my enemy or to touch my body with healing – you provide! If I need food, favor, friendship, or finances, you provide. Your provision has no limits!

So why? Why do I feel like I'm stuck between a rock and a hard place? Why do I panic when I don't know what to do? Wait. I know what to do. I'm supposed to seek you—to come to you—*first*. You still receive me even when I come to you third, fourth, or fifth. You're so good to me!

I come to you in fragility, and you provide me with courage and strength. I come to you in ignorance, and you give me answers to the questions I haven't even thought to ask. I approach you, broken and confused, and you shower me with clarity and boldness!

The boldness of the Lion of the Tribe of Judah is on my side! When I listen to you, I have confidence that the God of heaven and earth is watching over me and directing my footsteps. You give me the assurance that, no matter what I see with my eyes, you are working behind the scenes to reconstruct what was meant to take me out and use it to put me IN!

Lord, I can't fix this. But you can!

I release my hands from this state of affairs, and I give it all into your faithful and capable hands! Thank you, Jesus, for being there for me!

God's Word

"That's why I take pleasure in my weaknesses,
and in the insults, hardships, persecutions,
and troubles that I suffer for Christ.
For when I am weak, then I am strong."
—2 Corinthians 12:10 NLT

"And my God will supply every need of yours
according to his riches in glory in Christ Jesus."
—Philippians 4:19 ESV

"Do not worry then, saying,
'What will we eat?' or 'What will we drink?'
or 'What will we wear for clothing?'
For the Gentiles eagerly seek all these things;
for your heavenly Father knows that you need all these
things. But seek first His kingdom and
His righteousness, and all these things
will be added to you."
—Matthew 6:31-33 NASB

WORSHIP FIRST

Hi God. From the moment I get out of bed, I feel like I'm behind: *Hurry! Rush! Go!*

Breakfast? No time.

Workout? I'll do that before bed.

Pray? In the car on the way.

Perform well. Don't let anybody down. Pick up. Be prepared. Go, go, GO!

And yet all you want is me: a conversation with me; to hear my heart. You want me to confide in you about how I'm barely keeping my head above water. You're aching to throw me a life preserver of peace, happiness, and wisdom beyond what I could ever come up with myself.

Why? Why won't I worship before I work?

Martha did the same thing in Luke 10. She was getting ready for the meeting: putting out the bagels and making her agenda. She had her "to do" list, her productivity software was up-to-date, and she had finished her journaling. This breakneck speed is what the world is pushing us towards each day: it's all about planning, setting goals, and productivity.

All those things are good. But we can't be *truly* productive without the Creator of the Universe on our side. If we're preparing without involving God, we may be preparing for the wrong things!

So, Martha prepared. She got the food. She did the business. She felt really frustrated with Mary—and told Jesus about it, too. She sobbed, *"Mary's not helping me, and I'm doing all the work! I can't do this all by myself!"*

Jesus basically tells Martha, *"I never asked you to do it by yourself, sweetie. You just got out ahead of me."*

If I'm missing some peace, it's probably because I forgot to worship you before I worked. If I wait until the end of the day, I don't give you my best; I give you what's leftover. I need you involved at the *front end* before I have the opportunity to get distracted. I need your input. After all, maybe this is the right goal, but the wrong time. Maybe I'm planning for something *you* don't have planned.

What *is* your plan?

I want to be aware of you. I want to focus intentionally, relax, and bring my mind back into control. You're trying to tell me something . . .but am I really listening? God, you already have a great plan for me. I will resist all the other clamor. I *do* have a choice!

God's Word

"The Lord is my strength and my song,
And He has become my salvation;
This is my God, and I will praise Him;
My father's God, and I will exalt Him."
—Exodus 15:2 AMP

"Since, then, you have been raised with Christ,
set your hearts on things above, where Christ is,
seated at the right hand of God. Set your minds
on things above, not on earthly things."
—Colossians 3:1-2 NIV

"Surely goodness and mercy and unfailing love shall
follow me all the days of my life, and I shall dwell
forever [throughout all my days] in the house
and in the presence of the Lord."
—Psalm 23:6 AMP

I WANT CONTROL BACK

Hi God. That grouchy lady at the checkout counter is on my last nerve. And can you believe how long that red light was? That's ridiculous!

Hold up. I'm letting a perfect stranger (*ahem . . . an imperfect stranger*) and even inanimate objects, like that stoplight, determine whether or not I'm happy. I don't trust those people with my feelings! Did you see the nasty look on her face? I don't even know her! I don't want her sour-faced finger in control of whether or not I'm having a good day!

That's it! I'm taking back CONTROL of my happiness! It's a decision, not a feeling. It's a *click* in my heart and my mind, not a magical moment when the whole world lines up. If the condition of my contentment is based on everyone else getting it right . . . I'm screwed! Game over!

I'm taking it back! Happiness is mine! I can be happy ANYWHERE, in any circumstance, if I'm in you and you're in me. I'm not alone. And honestly, I've seen people in worse circumstances than me be happier than me!

If they can be happy in a really yucky place, I can put on my *"happy pants"* and get glad in the same pants I got mad in. The expression on my face and my positive attitude prove that my love and faith in you is unconditional!

True happiness isn't where I live or who I hang out with. Real joy doesn't come from a dollar amount or a number of "followers." Regardless of how I feel in my body, how people are treating me, how messy the house is, or how bad the car is acting . . . real happiness comes from believing you are who you say you are!

It's time! I'm not going to let my emotions control me anymore! I'm going to control them! And that will lead me to the strongest place in my life! The joy of the Lord is my strength! Happiness based on "them," or joy based on YOU? I pick option two!

You know how everything ends. If you're not worried . . . why should I be? That's so silly, it's worth laughing at! I give up my frown and turn it around. It's time to put on my *crown of happiness!* I let the strength of your method of operation give me the strength I've always wanted!

I've got control back!

God's Word

"Though the fig tree does not bud and there are
no grapes on the vines, though the olive crop fails
and the fields produce no food, though there are
no sheep in the pen and no cattle in the stalls,
yet I will rejoice in the Lord, I will be joyful in God
my Savior. The Sovereign Lord is my strength;
he makes my feet like the feet of a deer,
he enables me to tread on the heights."
—Habakkuk 3:17-19 NIV

"Honor and majesty surround him; strength
and joy fill his dwelling."
—1 Chronicles 16:27 NLT

"Heaven-throned God breaks out laughing.
At first he's amused at their presumption."
—Psalm 2:4 MSG

I'M SO EMBARRASSED

Hi God. I don't know what I'm going to do if they find out. I can't tell them. There's NO WAY they're going to understand. But I think they might know. How do I face them? I didn't mean . . . it wasn't supposed to . . . I couldn't make it stop. I still can't believe it myself!

That's not me. It WAS me. But it isn't me anymore. I'm not sure why would anyone else ever believe that?

I can feel people looking at me when I walk into a room. Something like that wasn't supposed to be a part of my story. Why do they keep staring? I'm distracted by it all, and petrified that it'll only get worse!

I bring this to you. I know you've forgiven me, even though I don't think I've been able to forgive myself all the way yet. YOUR understanding, somehow, is easier to take than their empty stares. YOUR forgiveness is so deep and fast. It's like a tsunami that rushes over me as soon as I open the gates of repentance.

But THEM . . ..

I need your help to tame this *"shame game"*. You didn't create me, send Jesus to die for me, and forgive me just for me to hide from everyone for the rest of my life. You don't shame me, and you don't want shame to lame me.

Somehow, you take what was meant to be shame and change it to honor. Like water to wine. The physics don't make sense, but that doesn't stop you. It's the promise you've given me.

- I thought it was my tombstone, but you made it my stepping stone.
- I thought it was my end, and somehow, you made it my beginning.
- I thought it would make me lame, and somehow, someway, my life is never going to be the same because of your grace!

You close the mouths of the lions. You elevate the lowly. You gave my shame to Jesus to wear on the cross. And in return, I get to take His coat of honor and drape it over my shoulders. I don't deserve it.

And that is the beauty of you. You take the repentant and undeserving and cover them in a grace that I can't fathom. You give me a shame-stripping honor that makes no sense, except to you.

Thank you, Father! Help me be more like you!

God's Word

"Instead of your shame you shall have double honor, and instead of confusion they shall rejoice in their portion. Therefore in their land they shall possess double; everlasting joy shall be theirs."
—Isaiah 61:7 KJV

"As it is written: 'Behold, I lay in Zion a stumbling stone and rock of offense, and whoever believes on Him will not be put to shame.'"
—Romans 9:33 NKJV

"Looking unto Jesus, the author and finisher of our faith, who for the joy that was set before Him endured the cross, despising the shame, and has sat down at the right hand of the throne of God."
—Hebrews 12:2 NKJV

"I counsel you to buy from Me gold refined in the fire, that you may be rich; and white garments, that you may be clothed, that the shame of your nakedness may not be revealed; and anoint your eyes with eye salve, that you may see."
—Revelation 3:18 NKJV

DREAM DELAY

Hi God. I'm really excited about the way things have been going. I heard your voice. I got the idea. The dream came alive and the door starting opening. I was so psyched!

I was thinking things were going to *pop* any second . . .like, any second . . .maybe now. Okay, NOW! Because, honestly, I thought it would be done by now . . . or even last month.

This dream seems like it's on "delay." I planted the seed. I'm believing you. I watered the seed in faith and prayer. What's happening?

I wonder if Noah felt the same way when you told him to build the ark. What a world-rocking dream! I can't imagine how excited he was when he knew that this vision, this desire, and this call on his life to invent the first boat ever built was going to happen.

And then, according to Jewish tradition, he planted the seeds to the trees that would grow and provide the wood he would cut down to make the boat. Hold up! That's a decades-long dream delay! Wait for trees to grow? I want to buy the pre-built dream!

What did he do wrong? Was he being punished? Did Noah make you mad? No. The Bible doesn't say any of that. This was just part of the process.

Noah did all you commanded, including being patient in the process and not getting discouraged while things developed.

Maybe that's what I need to do. Instead of going on a witch-hunt of what could possibly be wrong, when things don't hum along as quickly and easily as I imagined they would . . . I just need to trust your timing.

I know that you're on my side. I know that you're working on things for me, whether I can see them or not. So why am I getting antsy? You're a right-on-time, at-the-RIGHT-time kind of God!

If there's a delay, it's because you're working something out, growing big strong trees, lining things up, and making things better!

You don't delay dreams. You prepare and train me, from the very onset of the dream seed, so that I not only get the dream, but I get to KEEP the dream! Thank you, God, for helping me understand that a big harvest takes a while to grow.

God's Word

"Make yourself an ark of gopherwood;
make rooms in the ark, and cover it inside and outside
with pitch. And this is how you shall make it:
The length of the ark shall be three hundred cubits,
its width fifty cubits, and its height thirty cubits."
—Genesis 6:14-15 NKJV

"Noah did everything God commanded him to do."
—Genesis 6:22 MSG

"The Lord is not slow in keeping his promise,
as some understand slowness. Instead he is patient
with you, not wanting anyone to perish,
but everyone to come to repentance."
—2 Peter 3:9 NIV

"Therefore say to them, 'Thus says the Lord God:
"None of My words will be postponed any more,
but the word which I speak will be done,"
says the Lord God.'"
—Ezekiel 12:28 NKJV

I DON'T FEEL
THE LOVE

Hi God. They say you're here, but I don't feel you. I mean, seriously. What does it take to "feel the love"? I know you wouldn't leave me. It's me that wanders off from you. I don't want to be stuck out here without you. Could I make you love me again?

But the truth is I can't ever walk out of the love of God! I can walk out of your will, or walk right out of your blessing. I can walk out of your way – but your love follows me, WHEREVER I go!

The prodigal son took all he had and left his father. He might have left his father, but his father's love never left him. Even when the son was at his lowest point, his father was waiting for him to come home. Not to be made fun of. Not to be ridiculed . . . but to be reinstated.

Isn't it funny that the son who was home the whole time didn't "feel the love" either? This must be a normal trick of the enemy. He was taken care of, provided for, and living the good life. And somehow, he was still jealous when his brother returned home and got some attention.

Is that what I do, God? Do I think you don't love me because it looks to me like you treat other people better than you treat me? That's a mess! Geez, I don't want to be THAT guy!

You said that nothing will shake your love for me. Not jealousy. Not stupidity. Not sin. NO chasm of time or space. You're going to love me through it all, regardless of how I feel.

Love isn't a feeling, it's a fact when it comes to you. Love is what I'm supposed to be rooted and grounded in. When I'm anchored in your love (whether I feel it or not), that love gives me power!

The power to be more like you, the God of love. The power to love more like you, and help others feel it. Love is what I've been wanting, and it's the very thing you're calling me to give. What I give, I get. Wait! If I give your love . . . I'll begin to feel your love!

This whole time, I've made this about me . . . and really, it's about your other kids. But when I make it about your other kids, I get what I want, too! You're amazing! God, help me to love more like you!

God's Word

"'Though the mountains be shaken and the hills
be removed, yet my unfailing love for you will not be
shaken nor my covenant of peace be removed,'
says the Lord, who has compassion on you."
—Isaiah 54:10 NIV

"And the son said to him, 'Father, I have sinned
against heaven and before you. I am no longer worthy
to be called your son.' But the father said to his
servants, 'Bring quickly the best robe, and put it
on him, and put a ring on his hand, and shoes on
his feet. And bring the fattened calf and kill it, and
let us eat and celebrate. For this my son was dead,
and is alive again; he was lost, and is found.'
And they began to celebrate."
—Luke 15:21-24 ESV

"For I am convinced that neither death nor life,
neither angels nor demons, neither the present nor the
future, nor any powers, neither height nor depth, nor
anything else in all creation, will be able to separate us
from the love of God that is in Christ Jesus our Lord."
—Romans 8:38-39 NIV

I DON'T WANT
TO WAIT!

Hi God.

Wait!

Hurry up and wait!

Wait your turn!

I'm just gonna be honest: I don't like waiting. I pick the shortest line at the grocery store on purpose! Ain't nobody got time for that!

Why wait? Why not now? I'm ready. Seriously— OVER-ready!

I'm ready for that job. I'm beyond ready for that house. God, I can totally handle that relationship, right now. My body needs to be healed, NOW! I need what's next. It's my turn! Right now, I'm going in circles, feeling crazy, just . . .waiting.

Speaking of circles, why did the Israelites have to walk around Jericho seven times before the walls fell? Couldn't that have happened on circle number one? It just took more time. More praise. More prayer. More faith. Hey, wait a minute!

I guess, my TV can be *on-demand* but my God can't. You're not Uber Eats, at my beck and call. You're the Creator of the Universe, who is merciful enough to have a conversation with me, one of seven billion humans. I think, maybe, my perspective got a little off.

Thank you, for listening to me when I pray. I honestly can't believe you take the time and effort to move things around on the earth on my behalf. You don't owe me anything . . . and I owe you, well, every single thing, including this moment.

Forgive me for forgetting how special our relationship is. If you have me in a holding pattern, it must not be safe to land. You have the big picture in mind. I only have right now in my sights.

Wait. You want me to wait? I'll do it—with a refocused vision and a tuned-up attitude. Thank you, God, for doing so much more for me that I have the ability to perceive. You aren't lazy; you're wise. I'll wait for that wisdom.

I'll wait and praise you. I'll wait with my hands held high in a beautiful mix of surrender and expectation. I'll wait on the God who does not fail. I'll wait with my hopes high and my confidence fixed on you!

You know what? I just realized waiting on you isn't so bad. I won't let a ticking clock hold more weight than my God. You're my Father, and you're working it all out for me!

God's Word

"I remain confident of this: I will see the goodness
of the LORD in the land of the living.
Wait for the LORD; be strong and take heart
and wait for the Lord."
—Psalm 27:13-14 NIV

"By faith the walls of Jericho fell, after the army
had marched around them for seven days."
—Hebrews 11:30 NIV

"The Lord is good to those who wait for him,
to the soul who seeks him."
—Lamentations 3:25 ESV

IN THE BLINK
OF AN EYE

Hi God. I can't believe they're gone! It's kind of surreal, and I'm not even positive what I'm feeling yet. A little numb. A bit like it isn't real. Then tears. Like something has been taken from me. Then a tendency to *buck up* and be strong. It feels like I'm trying to lean into my own strength and it's fake. And maybe . . .I'm even a little mad!

All this might seem so weird to you. I mean, I know Heaven is the most beautiful place that exists. I know they're living in a place that has no sickness, no disease, no hatred, no hurt . . . it doesn't even get dark at night. The temperature is always perfect! Their body has been glorified and they don't even have to go to the gym. Not to mention, the *Marriage Supper of the Lamb*. All that food and no workout required!

Okay . . . comic relief for a second. But I already miss them again. I can't believe I've lost them! But I haven't "lost" them; I know exactly where they are! To be absent from the body is to be present with the Lord! They're in Heaven with you! I've just never been there so it's hard for me to conceive of that place.

But Heaven is REAL. I've never been to Timbuktu, but it's real—with deserts and museums and cafes. I've never been to Antarctica, but it's all ice shelves, glaciers, and penguins there.

Just because I haven't seen it . . . doesn't mean it isn't real. This is when I have to trust you to take care of them better than I can. But who's going to take care of me??? Oh. Yeah. You. Okay, I'm blushing. I should have known that!

I'm going to miss them, desperately, but this isn't a forever goodbye. It's like they've moved to Antarctica— only warmer and more beautiful because it's HEAVEN! They've moved and I will see them again. When I move. Just not for a few years.

I can do this, Lord. I can trust you with my sweet loved one until I get to see them again. The funny thing is, they won't even get a chance to miss me. A day in heaven is like a thousand years on earth. To them, I'll be there in the blink of an eye! That's how much you care for them. They have everything! They have you in heaven.

None of this took you by surprise. You've been building a house for them in heaven, getting just the right furnishings, and getting everything ready for their arrival. You've been waiting for this amazing moment when they get to be with you.

Thank you, Jesus, for taking care of the people I love! Tell them I miss them and I'll be there before they can blink. And Lord, help me to lean into you when I miss them. I want to finish strong on the Earth in everything you have called me to do. I trust you!

God's Word

"We are confident, yes, well pleased rather
to be absent from the body and to be present
with the Lord."
—2 Corinthians 5:8 NKJV

"But do not overlook this one fact, beloved,
that with the Lord one day is as a thousand years,
and a thousand years as one day."
—2 Peter 3:8 ESV

"There will be no more night in the city, and they
will have no need for the light of a lamp or of the sun.
For the Lord God will shine on them,
and they will reign forever and ever."
—Revelation 22:5 BSB

"He will wipe every tear from their eyes, and there
will be no more death or sorrow or crying or pain.
All these things are gone forever."
—Revelation 21:4 NLT

MOUNTAIN FLAVOR

Hi God. I feel like I'm in a valley surrounded by mountains, and I've had to climb each one of them to get here.

When I look around the valley, it's full—full of people better than me, more active than me, more gifted than me, more determined than me. I feel like I'm just one leaf in a huge forest. How, how, HOW could you possibly even SEE me . . . much less care for me?

The Bible says that you're a farmer and talks about vines and wines. The vinedresser. You have dressed me. It's a fact. I've been robed in your righteousness. You're the glory and the lifter of my head. I've seen you in places in my life where I thought I was alone. But then you've literally been draped around me and there to pick me up.

It's so easy to forget, as I'm lying on the ground feeling insignificant, that I'm not. When I'm on the ground, you come and pick me up. Why? So you can care for me and help me be all you called me to be (and that's not what you called my neighbor to be). I have to stop and think about that for a minute.

Each side of every mountain produces a slightly different flavor in the grape. Exposure to the sun (or your son, the soil they're planted in, the rockiness and acidity, the winds of adversity . . . it all factors into the FLAVOR.

You made me a flavor that only comes from the mountains that I've been on. The places I've been. The winds and rains that I've stood in with you. Every life, every story, every person has a different and unique flavor. That's why there are many vineyards in one region. The flavor is different. They may look the same, but the product—the flavor—is unique, special, and desired!

I'm ready for the next part of my journey! I'm ready for the many new *flavors* you're adding to my life!

God's Word

"'I am a true sprouting vine, and the farmer who
tends the vine is my Father. He cares for the
branches connected to me by lifting and propping up
the fruitless branches and pruning every
fruitful branch to yield a greater harvest.'"
—John 15:1-2 TPT

"I am overwhelmed with joy in the Lord my God!
For he has dressed me with the clothing of salvation
and draped me in a robe of righteousness.
I am like a bridegroom dressed for his wedding
or a bride with her jewels."
—Isaiah 61:10 NLT

"I praise you because I am fearfully and
wonderfully made; your works are wonderful,
I know that full well."
—Psalm 139:14 NIV

WRESTLING WITH GOD

Hi God. Look. You don't have to be so tough. I "get" wrestling around for fun. It's all fun and games until somebody gets hurt. But it looks like I'm the "somebody." *Uncle*, already!!! Let me out!

Sometimes, I don't like to pray, because I'm afraid of what you're going to say. I *hear* what you're saying . . . but it doesn't always make the most sense.

I didn't get the answer I wanted from you, so I asked a friend. They didn't have any answers, so I asked another friend. They told me, "You do what God is telling you to do." Well, that's just GREAT!!! Now, I'm fresh out of friends to ask. I guess I'll have to actually do what you're telling me to do!

I get it: Be willing and open for what God wants for me. With God, it's never for less, it's always for much MORE!

Your way is always going to be better than my way. If I could just stop wrestling with you for a minute . . . perhaps you'll show me why. God, you always have your reasons. I just can't always see them.

If Jacob had been successful when he wrestled in the womb, he would have been born in the wrong order. The *younger* will be served by the *older*. He would have gotten what he THOUGHT he wanted and lost his blessing.

Sometimes, it looks like we lose . . . but really, we WIN! That's why I have to submit to you and not fight you so much. Jacob fought you a lot, too.

You came to bless him and he wrestled with you, anyway. He fought in rebellion and left with a limp. When all along, he could've just received what you had for him. I don't want to limp in rebellion! I don't want to fight you when you try to bless me!

I can humble myself or be humbled. I'm not going to keep trying to get my way by claiming submission while, deep down, I'm still trying to change things around me. I'm not going to pretend that I can't hear you.

You want the best for me—even better than I want for myself. So today, I tap out. Your way, God! Your wonderful way!

God's Word

"Now may the God of peace—who brought up from the dead our Lord Jesus, the great Shepherd of the sheep, and ratified an eternal covenant with his blood—may he equip you with all you need for doing his will. May he produce in you, through the power of Jesus Christ, every good thing that is pleasing to him. All glory to him forever and ever! Amen."
—Hebrews 13:20-21 NLT

"The Lord said to her, '[The founders of] two nations are in your womb, and the separation of two nations has begun in your body; the one people shall be stronger than the other, and the older shall serve the younger.' When her days to be delivered were fulfilled, behold, there were twins in her womb.
The first came out reddish all over like a hairy garment, and they named him Esau (hairy).
Afterward, his brother came out, and his hand grasped Esau's heel, so he was named Jacob (one who grabs by the heel, supplanter). Isaac was sixty years old when Rebekah gave birth to them."
—Genesis 25:23-26 AMP

I DON'T WANT YOU TO SEE ME RIGHT NOW

Hi God. Sorry, my "FaceTime" isn't working . . . That isn't true. I just don't want you to see me right now. I'm not ready. Actually . . . I'm a mess! (And I don't mean that I have bed head.)

If I'm honest, I've been trying to avoid you altogether, because I don't want you to see me like this. I don't have my act together. I'm not proud of myself. And I don't want you to be disgusted by what you see if you glance my way. When I look at myself, I just shake my head. I don't even like what I see when I look at me.

I totally get why the Prodigal Son thought he couldn't go home. I can't imagine what it took to live in a pig pen and steal the pig's slop for food. My situation is bad, but I've never been *that* hungry and dirty. And still, he thought his dad wouldn't take him back . . . but he did!

I guess that's proof that you'll still accept me. When the son headed home, his father didn't yell at him and tell him how disappointed he was. He dropped everything and went running TO him. The father wasn't disgusted by the dirty son. He was just happy he was home—so happy that he threw him a party he didn't deserve!

That's you! You told that story because you're trying to help me understand YOU. I thought of you as judgmental, like me. But you just aren't. You aren't waiting to yell at me when we get together. You're waiting to hug me!

Jesus didn't go to the cross to keep us apart. He endured all my sin so that I would never have to stay away from you, for any reason—even the 100 reasons I can think of now. I'm not going to waste that huge sacrifice!

Jesus, thank you for dying so that I could live. God, thank you for forgiving me when I wouldn't forgive myself. I don't want to be far away from you anymore! I'm coming home, Daddy! I know you'll take me as you find me. I know you won't leave me the way you found me. I was a mess. But now, I'm found. I'm HOME!

God's Word

"But we all, with open face beholding as in a glass the glory of the Lord, are changed into the same image from glory to glory, even as by the Spirit of the Lord."
—2 Corinthians 3:18 KJV

"They looked to Him and were radiant, And their faces were not ashamed. Those who look to him are radiant; their faces are never covered with shame."
—Psalm 34:5 NKJV

"'I am no longer worthy to be called your son; make me like one of your hired servants.' So he got up and went to his father. But while he was still a long way off, his father saw him and was filled with compassion for him; he ran to his son, threw his arms around him and kissed him. The son said to him, 'Father, I have sinned against heaven and against you. I am no longer worthy to be called your son.' But the father said to his servants, 'Quick! Bring the best robe and put it on him. Put a ring on his finger and sandals on his feet.'"
—Luke 15:19-22 NIV

THE DRIVER'S SEAT

Hi God. I need to talk to you about the way things are going. I mean, we're off schedule here. Let me show you. Here are my goals and my calendar. These just don't match with what's happening!

I'm supposed to be further along by now: Married. Kids. House. Career. Not to mention, I'm supposed to be looking great in a swimsuit by now. I made a plan. I've been trying to work the plan. And HELLO . . . this ain't the plan!

What in the world happened? I thought I was in the driver's seat of my life. I thought I had it under control. But as I think about it, actually, Jesus is supposed to take the wheel. I'm supposed to be following your godly navigation, not trying to plot my own course.

Wow! No wonder I don't have any peace. It makes sense, now, why this seems so hard. I finally get why it seems like I keep progressing one exit up in life and then . . . BOOM! I keep getting forced into a U-turn. It's because I'm in the wrong position and driving full-speed ahead, without giving you the wheel.

Planning more without you doesn't fix it. I've tried that. That just makes you mad. What does it take for you to get invited to the planning meeting? How could I have missed that?

You didn't design me to be able to see the future. You're the Alpha and Omega. You are as much in my future as you are in my present. You know every twist and turn. You've routed me around challenges, pitfalls, and potholes. But the route only works if I take it.

If I keep insisting on my way, it's as if I'm placing myself ahead of you. If I try to make it myself, it's like I'm trying to lift myself up. You're happy to let me try that . . . but it gets me nowhere!

If I can commit to following the path and plan that you have for my life (even though it's a road I don't recognize), you'll take me through to a good place. Your plans for me are better than any plans I could ever make for myself.

Okay, God! Let's plan next year. What do you have in mind?

God's Word

"Commit your way to the Lord, trust also
in Him, and He shall bring it to pass."
—Psalm 37:5 NKJV

"I know what I'm doing. I have it all planned out—
plans to take care of you, not abandon you,
plans to give you the future you hope for."
—Jeremiah 29:11 MSG

"We can make our plans, but the Lord
determines our steps."
—Proverbs 16:9 NLT

I'M MAD

Hi God. I am so MAD right now! I want to spit, yell, cuss (I know I shouldn't cuss, but I'm just so angry), and throw a fit. I mean, *anybody* would—what happened is just NOT fair. It's not right!

Part of me wants to tell the whole world what a jerk that person is; the other part of me wants revenge. I want to make sure they don't treat anyone else like this ever again. I would *never* do anything like this. Well, at least not intentionally . . . or unintentionally. I just wouldn't! I'm not that kind of person.

Yeah, I know I've done things I didn't mean to do. At times, my words have come out much stronger than they should have come out. And there were a few times when I reacted too fast and a little (just a little) too harshly. But this is . . . different!

How is it different? It's different because . . . I wouldn't have done *that*! At least, not that way. It's different because it happened to *me*!

Now that I think about it, I've done some pretty dumb stuff in my life. There are a few people that have "the right" to be ticked at me . . .including you. I've done plenty to aggravate you—even though I *try* to be good. I'm so glad you're not in heaven stomping around and yelling about how terrible I am. I would hate that.

I'm beginning to see how I'm letting anger turn me into someone I don't want to be: someone who's going to need grace and forgiveness myself.

God, if you got mad and flew off the handle at me, like I'm doing to this person . . . I wouldn't stand a chance. Thank you for not doing that. I know that, in order for me to receive your grace and forgiveness, I've got to give that forgiveness and grace to the people I'd rather scream at (obviously, I'm not as good at this as you are).

Help me, God, to calm down! Help me to walk in the peace that only comes from you. Help me to forgive this person (even though it's so hard to utter those words).

Help me to extend to this person the grace that I want from you—no, the grace I NEED from you! I turn this situation over to you, God. Have your way with both myself and this other person. I give them the forgiveness that I want in my life. It's a seed, Lord. And I believe I'll reap that same love back when I don't deserve it.

God's Word

"Be angry and do not sin; do not let the sun
go down on your anger."
—Ephesians 4:26 ESV

"Therefore, as God's chosen people, holy and
dearly loved, clothe yourselves with compassion,
kindness, humility, gentleness and patience.
Bear with each other and forgive one another if
any of you has a grievance against someone.
Forgive as the Lord forgave you."
—Colossians 3:12-13 NIV

"Never pay back evil for evil to anyone.
Respect what is right in the sight of all men.
If possible, so far as it depends on you,
be at peace with all men."
—Romans 12:17-18 NASB

THE MESS

Hi God. It seems like everybody only shares the *pretty* parts of their lives. You know, selfies taken once they're dressed up for the party; once the presents are wrapped and the tree is decorated. Those are the picture-perfect moments I see.

Sometimes, when I compare their amazing moments to my muddle, I forget that most of life isn't that picture-perfect for anyone! As a matter of fact, every Pinterest-perfect picture probably took hours to take (not to mention the 19 deleted photo fails before it).

When I see others and their expressions of happiness and success, I have a tendency to get frustrated with the fact that I look at myself and see . . .well, a *hot mess*!

Life gets messy in order to make a miracle moment. The miraculous doesn't manifest in the mainstream and the 'picture-perfect.' Your power is made perfect in my weakness. You move in areas that I can't. And when I see a cluttered and chaotic life, you see an opportunity to do something great.

Actually, right in the middle of all that confusion, you are probably already at work. I need to relax. Trust you.

Many times, making a mess in the present is preparation for the future. No home makeover was ever completed without first getting things dirty and disorganized. A mess in the kitchen simply means that a great meal is about to be served! A closet full of clutter simply reminds me of how blessed I am to have so much to share!

I'll learn to look beyond my mess. I will trust you, and allow what seems to be chaos to energize me. You're getting ready to show up. You have me in preparation mode. You have my remodel in progress! I will let this chaos be my friend. I will allow the preparation to be just as much fun as the payoff.

I make a decision, right now, to enjoy every single maddening moment of this season. I know that, if there's a mess in my life right now, you're busy arranging a tremendous miracle at the end of it! I declare, in the name of Jesus, that my future is beautiful beyond my wildest expectations! I'll drink in this disorganization and preparation, and see it as a blessing.

I will take a mental snapshot, God, because this is my *before* picture!

God's Word

"Let us not become conceited, or provoke one another, or be jealous of one another."
—Galatians 5:26 NLT

"Each time he said, 'My grace is all you need. My power works best in weakness.' So now I am glad to boast about my weaknesses, so that the power of Christ can work through me."
—2 Corinthians 12:9 NLT

"You shall not covet [that is, selfishly desire and attempt to acquire] your neighbor's house; you shall not covet your neighbor's wife, or his male servant, or his female servant, or his ox, or his donkey, or anything that belongs to your neighbor."
—Exodus 20:17 AMP

APPROVAL ADDICT

Hi God. Sometimes, I act so tough—like I can handle it all. Which is crazy, because most of the time, I don't even know what "it" is. Sometimes, it's a snappy comment on social media (why are Facebook users so mean? I thought they were my friends!). These comments are painful! And when they come from friends—or even worse, family—I'm undone!

Why does it only take one mean-spirited conversation, word, or comment (or worse, lack of a comment) to slay me? I act like I have the world in my hand—as if I'm in control. I act like their words don't matter. But it's just an *act*. They mean so much more than I want them to mean. It feels like those comments either confirm or deny that I should even be where I am today.

My need for validation is so misguided!

I'm not called to get *their* approval. As a matter of fact, if I do what really pleases you, there are a few feathers I'm going to ruffle. A few folks are going to be so surprised and unintentionally threatened that I'm going to need you as my backbone to continue.

You! That's the beauty of you! You are my covering and my strength. You're who I talk to, who I confide in, who I look for in a crowd. You're the one smile and nod that matters.

I could scan for the approval of my mom, my boss, my teacher, my coach, my mentor, or my spouse; but they may not care, or have enough courage to cheer me on. It's not because they don't love me, they just aren't equipped to handle what I'm called to just yet.

But you are. You're the One Who called me out of obscurity into your marvelous light! You! I want the approval of people, but I *need* your approval!

To be wanted by you is like air to my lungs and like fuel to my ability to continue. You're the energy I need to be who I am. I'm not who I am without you. I am who I am *because* of you!

Vulnerable is something I'm so hesitant to be. Because every time I have been . . . it hasn't turned out well. Until you! You are my safe place, my hiding place, my security, my cheerleader, and my encourager! You believe in me when I can't imagine why anyone would.

Right now, I just want to say, thank you! Thank you, for seeing through the façade. Thank you, for loving me, anyway. Thank you, for calling me beyond all that I could ever have hoped for. And Lord, help me to be all that you've called me to be!

God's Word

"I will say of the Lord, 'He is my refuge
and my fortress;
My God, in Him I will trust.'"
—Psalm 91:2 NKJV

"But you are a chosen generation, a royal
priesthood, a holy nation, His own special people,
that you may proclaim the praises of Him who called
you out of darkness into His marvelous light."
—1 Peter 2:9 NKJV

"Am I now trying to win the approval of
human beings, or of God? Or am I trying to please
people? If I were still trying to please people,
I would not be a servant of Christ."
—Galatians 1:10 NIV

GOING UNDER

Hi God. I'm surprised you didn't hear the sound of me gurgling when I said that. I've been trying to keep my head above water . . . and I'm not sure that I can!

I've been treading water for as long as I can, and it seems like the water is getting higher and higher. I can imagine what Peter felt like when he was "starting to sink." I'm still breathing, which means I'm not under . . . yet. I feel like I'm in the same place Peter was!

But even though Peter stopped having faith for a moment, you didn't let him sink. Your mercy and compassion overflowed when Peter cried, *"Lord, save me!"*

If it worked for him, it will work for me. I cry out to you, right now: *"Lord, save ME!"*

When Peter yelled those words, Jesus, you didn't hesitate. You came immediately. As I cry out these words, I know that you're with me, stretching out your hand to lift me up.

You won't let me fall. I know I need you. I know you are filled with mercy. I know that you died so I could live. The Bible tells me that you loved me first. Even when I fail you—and fail myself—my failure doesn't separate us. It simply gives me an opportunity to lean into your forgiveness and compassion. Your love for me is so much deeper than the troubles that surround me!

Jesus, you came to seek and save people just like me. I need you to save me! You're faithful. Faithful beyond measure. You don't even know how to break your Word.

You came—your Word came—to save me from situations just like this. Your life had a purpose: to SAVE! And you created my life to have purpose, as well.

My arms are open. My faith is renewed and I'm reaching up to you. Thank you, God, for saving me!

God's Word

"But when he saw that the wind was boisterous,
he was afraid; and beginning to sink he cried out,
saying, 'Lord, save me!' And immediately Jesus
stretched out His hand and caught him,
and said to him, 'O you of little faith,
why did you doubt?'"
—Matthew 14:30-31 NKJV

"For the Son of Man came to seek and
save those who are lost."
—Luke 19:10 NLT

"He sent out his word and healed them,
snatching them from the door of death."
—Psalm 107:20 NLT

AM I FIGHTING THE WRONG FIGHT?

Hi God. I thought I was right. I mean, to be honest, I'm still not sure that I was wrong. Yet here we are, stuck in the middle of a mess that I'd love to blame on someone else. In fact, in my mind, I've already blamed them. But when we're alone—just you and me—I know.

You've already told me what to show other people: Honor. Forgiveness. Love. Kindness. Obedience. But then, things get off-kilter and it seems like I *know* how to get in there and shore things up. *I can help!* In these moments, I feel like I know exactly what I'm doing.

Then, things start going south and everything turns into such a confusing mess. I think I'm fighting to be the voice of reason in these situations, but I can't be the voice of reason *and* be in strife at the same time. I need to recognize what strife truly looks like. You didn't call me to be a strife-bearer, a friction fan, or someone always willing to fight to make it right. Most things don't matter that much . . .Not all fights are mine to wage or to win.

The one always wanting to stand up and fight is likely also the one who will often bring confusion and hurt into the situation. You actually demand that this person gets kicked out. I don't want to be kicked out . . . My heart is, truly, to help.

You tell me to forgive. Forgive when they are wrong. Forgive when they can't see it. Forgive when their words are sideways or they're doing it wrong (at least, in my opinion). My job isn't to make everything right, come up with the answer, or push the boulder up the hill. My job is to bring peace, to speak love, to help through healing—not simply to stand up for one side and bring division.

I've had the right heart, but the wrong approach. Lord, thank you for helping me see how I've been hurting instead of helping. Your loving guidance will help me help other people. Your corrections will keep the confusion and hurt from blindsiding me so often.

The enemy has been using me against myself, trying to keep me in a whirlwind of winning the wrong way. I lay down the plan of my flesh and pick up the tools of love, peace, understanding, wisdom, and forgiveness. I'm now armed to make a difference – the *right* way!

God's Word

"Drive out a scoffer, and strife will go out,
and quarreling and abuse will cease."
—Proverbs 22:10 ESV

"Then Peter came to Jesus and asked,
'Lord, how many times shall I forgive my brother
who sins against me? Up to seven times?'
Jesus answered, 'I tell you, not just seven times,
but seventy-seven times!'"
—Matthew 18:21-22 NIV

"If it is possible, as far as it depends on you,
live at peace with everyone."
—Romans 12:18 NIV

ARE YOU EVEN HERE?

Hi God. Where are you? I can't see you. I can't see where you've been. When I look back over my life, there have been many times I've needed you there . . . but I'm not sure that you were there.

I'm looking—I mean, really LOOKING—for you. I see you sometimes, like when I pray for a parking space, or when I need to get through something quickly. And you must show up because these things happen. But . . .where are you during the other times?

I can see the problems clearly: The bill collector calls, but the person I love won't. There are people all around me, but I still feel lonely. I'm trying to wade through this on my own, but I just feel outnumbered, out-classed, and it looks as if the enemy has more firepower than I do.

I try to walk by faith and not by sight. But I see the enemy swarming and circling. They seem to be moving faster and closing in.

Just because I can't see you doesn't mean I'm alone in this. *The Invisible Hand of God* is lining things up for me. Every now and then, I get a glimpse of the fourth man in the fire: a slight hint of a look at your fingerprints. But they aren't the proof. They're just what's left behind.

Moses couldn't *see* God. But you still held back the Red Sea so the Israelites could pass safely.

David couldn't *see* God. But it didn't keep you from guiding his stone into the enemy's forehead.

Elisha couldn't *see* God. But you still caused the borrowed, lost axe head to float.

Daniel couldn't *see* God. But you still held the mouths of the lions closed.

The Israelites couldn't *see* God. But you still pushed over the walls of Jericho and gave them a victory when they didn't even have to fight.

God, I can't see you, but you're building my victory in the background. The Bible says you don't do for one person what you won't do for another.

So I'll stop looking for you with my natural eyes, and I'll stop *naturalizing* the situation. Instead, I'll open my spiritual eyes and see you moving and protecting me, in the Spirit.

Thank you, God, for working for me when I wasn't even looking!

"And I will ask the Father, and he will give you
another Counselor to be with you forever—
the Spirit of truth. The world cannot accept him,
because *it neither sees him* nor knows him. But you know
him, for he lives with you and will be in you."
—John 14:16-17 NIV

"And Peter opened his mouth and said:
Most certainly *and* thoroughly I now perceive
and understand that God shows no partiality
and is no respecter of persons."
—Acts 10:34 AMP

"For we walk by faith [we *regulate* our lives and conduct
ourselves by our conviction or belief respecting man's
relationship to God and divine things, with trust and
holy fervor; thus we walk] not by sight *or* appearance."
—2 Corinthians 5:7 AMP

WILL YOU?

Hi God. I'm out here by myself, and I really need your help. But then, I listen to what some people say, and I'm not sure if you *will* help me.

I'm not even close to being perfect. I mess up. I underperform. I sin. You have expectations for me, and I don't meet them. I try to *act* like a Christian. I try to *be* good. I try to *look* like I have it together. But I know, and you know, that's not true.

So why in the world would you help me? I don't deserve it; I haven't earned it.

I just don't GET you. You aren't like me. You aren't human. Your love and compassion are so deep that I could get lost in them for eternity! You love your enemies! I know I'm not your enemy, I'm your child. You're my Father. Your love for me must be some kind of crazy love!

You're not waiting for me to act right. You're waiting for me to ask in faith, believing that your goodness outweighs my failures. I'm confident that your grace is enough. You don't help me because I'm good. You help me because *you're* good!

Everybody wonders what your will is, or what you *will* do. I don't have to wonder: you tell me!

You say that you *will* strengthen me. You declare that you *will* uphold me. You *will* give me grace beyond my need. You *will* find me. You *will* help me. You *will* give me what I need!

I can't earn it. I don't deserve it. I can't be good enough. Righteousness comes with repentance. It's a *gift*. It's a present. Your gift of love lives in my present. And I love presents!

Jesus, I'm so sorry for operating outside of what you have asked me to do. Right now, I turn from those stinking words, sour attitudes, and stupid actions, and I run to you!

Now, standing in a position that is unwarranted, unmerited, and by human standards, *impossible*, I ask you by your heavenly promise to be with me. Guide me. Help me. Heal me. Forgive me. And lead me into your blessed and promised *will* for me!

God's Word

"Fear not, for I am with you; be not dismayed,
for I am your God. I will strengthen you, yes,
I will help you, I will uphold you with
My righteous right hand."
—Isaiah 41:10 NKJV

"And He said to me, 'My grace is sufficient for you,
for My strength is made perfect in weakness.'
Therefore most gladly I will rather boast
in my infirmities, that the power of Christ
may rest upon me."
—2 Corinthians 12:9 NKJV

"Ask and it will be given to you; seek and you will
find; knock and the door will be opened to you.
For everyone who asks receives; the one who seeks
finds; and to the one who knocks,
the door will be opened."
—Matthew 7:7-8 NIV

I WANT IT MY WAY

Hi God. Sometimes, I look at my situation and feel incredibly disappointed!

No one wakes up in the morning and says, "Hey, I'm going to ruin my life today." Nobody says, "I'm going to start a bad habit," or, "I'm going to lose my job," or, "I'm going to get a divorce." There isn't one person who has that kind of "To Do" list. But it happens all the time.

More than once, I've woken up with a plan to do things *my* way. But then, when I move toward my plan, the whole thing falls apart! I'm left feeling down, discouraged, and depressed, thinking, "What happened?"

When something goes wrong, I just want to put my head down and hide. Right in the middle of those feelings of disappointment, freaking out, loss, overwhelming loneliness, and exhausting defeat, it seems like my happy life is over.

But God . . . How many times have I suffered a deep disappointment, only for you to set up a *new* appointment to take its place?

You have arranged a fresh reappointment for me on the other side of this sadness. You, somehow, make *all things* (even the painful breakup of a relationship or a great job disappearing) work together for my good! Only you.

God, if I had continued with my original plan, you would never have been able to reappoint me to an exciting new season of opportunity.

We can make our plans, but the LORD determines our steps.

I have to remember *that with you*, every disappointment will ultimately result in a new and better reappointment. Only with you are all things are possible!

Just because events don't go my way doesn't mean I have to let them change my day. I'll simply make a *new* "To Do" list:

- I'll confess faith in you instead of fear or doubt.
- I will proclaim that "I can" instead of "I can't."
- I'll believe for blessing instead of expecting lack.
- I'll declare victory instead of hurrying to admit weakness or defeat.

God, your unique perspective sees the beginning from the end. I may not understand everything but I will trust you. Trusting you is the first step to moving beyond these negative feelings.

God, you already know how you're going to turn this disappointment around. Thank you, for making it one of the most AMAZING highlights of my life! I will hang on to see what you will do—because I know it's going to be awesome!

God's Word

"For as the heavens are higher than the earth,
so are My ways higher than your ways, and My
thoughts than your thoughts."
—Isaiah 55:9 NKJV

"The LORD directs the steps of the godly.
He delights in every detail of their lives."
—Psalm 37:23 NLT

"And we know that for those who love God all things
work together for good, for those who are called
according to his purpose."
—Romans 8:28 ESV

I'M READY TO FIGHT

Hi God. They want to fight! Okay - let's go! I'm down to defend my honor. I'm up to standing up for myself. I'm not going to let them take advantage of me like this!

They come at me swinging, and I'm not gonna back down. I'll come at them like a spider monkey! Right, God? Right? God???

You're not saying anything. Your echo of support would be awesome right now. Still nothing?

Why?

I know you call me to fight my battles in prayer. I know that if I come at them *in the flesh*, I'll have to defeat them *in the flesh*. If I come at them like they come at me, I'm no better than they are. And, the only weapons I'll have are the same weapons they have.

Okay. This is starting to make sense. My weapons aren't flesh and blood. My fight isn't fists and blows. My fight isn't harsh words and strife. My fight isn't "you hit me and I'll hit you harder."

My fight is the fight of FAITH. It's the fight I fight to keep from fighting. I fight in the Spirit. And the flesh cannot stand against the spiritual realm. Either, I trust in my strength, my ideas, and strategies, and in the counsel and brawn of my friends . . . or I trust in you.

I turn my enemies over to you, and I call out their names in prayer. I take counsel with the *Lion of the Tribe of Judah* and loose your judgment on them (even if your judgment is grace—*gulp*!) God, you've gotta be my backup on this. This is a new way of fighting for me.

I don't sling curse words. You call me to sling words of blessing on my enemies. To L-L-L-LOVE them. Okay, that kinda made me stutter.

But when I fight your way, I get your favor. I have the assurance of your strength. I have all of Heaven's armies working with me.

You didn't leave David *out to dry* when he ran toward Goliath. Moses and the Israelites were safe because they did it your way. You made Elijah look good when he took on 400 prophets of Baal. And you're going to do the same for me!

The battle is yours, God! I'm fighting your way!

God's Word

"For every child of God defeats this evil world,
and we achieve this victory through our faith.
And who can win this battle against the world?
Only those who believe that Jesus is the Son of God."
—1 John 5:4-5 NLT

"For we do not wrestle against flesh and blood,
but against principalities, against powers, against the
rulers of the darkness of this age, against spiritual
hosts of wickedness in the heavenly places."
—Ephesians 6:12 NKJV

"Jesus said to him, 'Put your dagger away.
For all those who embrace violence
will die by violence.'"
—Matthew 26:52 TPT

"Fight the good fight of the faith. Take hold of the
eternal life to which you were called and about
which you made the good confession in the
presence of many witnesses."
—1 Timothy 6:12 ESV

WHAT MORE DO YOU WANT FROM ME?

Hi God. Look. Let's just get to it. What more do you want from me? I mean, I TRY. Nothing seems good enough. I give to you and it seems you want more. I've changed for the better, in so many ways, but it feels like there's more you think I could do.

I help people (sometimes). I'm kind (kinder than I used to be). I give (not as much as I could, but I'm way more generous than I used to be). I mean, people NOTICE the change in me. Why, why, WHY do you want MORE??? It feels unfair.

Abraham might have felt the same way. Ninety-nine years of waiting, and do you bless him? No. You give him a covenant and require a "cutting." No positive pregnancy test after nine decades. Just a requirement of circumcision for him AND everyone in his house. I bet that went over like a ton of bricks at the family meeting!

Why do you want more from me when I'm ready for something from you? I guess you want to see if I'm serious about you or just looking for what I can get out of the relationship. I bet you need to know that I can handle the blessing and not lose my mind. And, I just realized, you need SEED to produce my harvest.

God, do you want to see if you can take EVERYTHING from me? Why? Because you return it to me, but so much better - with blessing! What if you asked me to give everything I have ever wanted and dreamed of? Can I posture myself in a position of humility and trust?

You've already shown me the precedent. Jesus had a protocol. The boy gave him five loaves and two fish and he blessed it, broke it, and gave it. When Jesus sat down at the Last Supper, he did the same thing with that bread -- right before he blessed, broke, and gave his body on the cross. You just want to know if I can do the same.

You want to know if I can stop relying on my own ability and give control back to you. You. Faithful. Restorer. Blesser. Lover of my Soul. You, who only wants it so that you can bless it and give it back to me.

What have I been waiting for, Lord? What do you want from me? It's yours!

God's Word

"'I will establish my covenant as an everlasting covenant between me and you and your descendants after you for the generations to come, to be your God and the God of your descendants after you. The whole land of Canaan, where you now reside as a foreigner, I will give as an everlasting possession to you and your descendants after you; and I will be their God.' Then God said to Abraham, 'As for you, you must keep my covenant, you and your descendants after you for the generations to come. This is my covenant with you and your descendants after you, the covenant you are to keep: Every male among you shall be circumcised. You are to undergo circumcision, and it will be the sign of the covenant between me and you.'"
—Genesis 17:7-11 NIV

"And he directed the people to sit down on the grass. Taking the five loaves and the two fish and looking up to heaven, he gave thanks and broke the loaves. Then he gave them to the disciples, and the disciples gave them to the people."
—Matthew 14:19 NIV

THAT'S NOT
MY NAME

Hi God. I can't believe they called me that. How RUDE!!! Didn't their momma teach them better manners? How could they say that about me? It's so far from the truth! My momma doesn't dress me funny! She doesn't even dress me . . .anymore.

But if all those crazy-hurtful names aren't true (oh, and they're NOT) then why does it sting so badly? It kind of makes me wonder . . .Do they see something in me I don't see? Could it be possible that I am who they say I am? Is there some shred of truth in what seems to be lies?

Hold up! I think the enemy is using my brain for a playground. One little seed and he's going to town. I know who I am because you told me! You not only told me who I am . . . you NAMED me!

Just like Jacob. His momma named him "trickster and supplanter." That had to hurt—every time he was on the playground, or even at the office, years later. But you, God, have the power to change my name.

Who I was before you, and who I am with you, are two completely different people. They are so far apart! After you came into my heart, I had to introduce myself to myself. I was transformed, saved, set free, purposed, made new, loved and redeemed. I have a whole new set of names from you!

Part of my name comes from you, Papa. Abba Father, you sprinkled some of your names in me. Your names are majestic. Your names are many because just one name can't contain you. I'm born of you, created by you, and intended because of you.

I can listen to what the enemy calls me, in the echoes of my mind, and allow him to name me. Or . . . I can shut him down and praise you for all the amazing names you've given me as your blessed child, your friend, your masterpiece!

The next time somebody tries to name me, blame me, shame me, or maim me with a name that isn't mine, I'll remember the names you, my Father God, gave me. Blessed! Healed! Delivered! Child of the Most High King! Restored! Righteous through Christ! That's quite a long name to learn to spell in kindergarten . . . but I like it!

"And He said, 'Your name shall no longer be Jacob, but Israel; for you have struggled with God and with men and have prevailed.' Then Jacob asked Him, 'Please tell me Your name.' But He said, 'Why is it that you ask My name?' And He declared a blessing [of the covenant promises] on Jacob there."
—Genesis 32:28-29 AMP

"Listen to me, O coastlands, and give attention, you peoples from afar. The LORD called me from the womb, from the body of my mother he named my name."
—Isaiah 49:1 ESV

"No longer do I call you servants, for the servant does not know what his master is doing; but I have called you friends, for all that I have heard from my Father I have made known to you."
—John 15:15 ESV

A MENTAL PRISON

Hi God. I'm walking around, out and about, in the free world with everyone else. So why does it feel like there are these barriers, these walls, these borders I can't get past? Why does it feel like I'm in a prison with no walls?

If what's going on in the world, or *my* world, goes a little off-plan, I end up hurt, sometimes confused, and upset. I HATE that feeling! That's the feeling of the enemy trying to steal my blessing.

The enemy has an opportunity to lead my life when I hold a grudge, justify anger, work myself up, or cultivate bitterness. He wants to trap me in frustration and my emotions and keep me bound by the very things I vow that I have the right to feel. He stands there with the keys and tries to convince me I'm better off where I am.

Why would I defend my right to suffer? Satan is the *father of lies* and the jailer of my happiness.

The enemy is NOT my leader!

He would lead me right into a mental prison.

My leader is God!

My leader is LOVE!

You lead me to freedom and peace!

There's an opportunity to break the chains that are binding me to my pain so that I can go where I'm trying to go without getting stuck in my past. There's one weapon that works against hatred and hurt, offense and fear. There's one key that unlocks that door. And that one key is love! Outrageous LOVE!

You can try to put me in a prison of feelings, justifications, and emotions, but I can still CHOOSE to be free! Love opens the door. Love sets me free!

Jesus loved me so much that the only time he let a prisoner remain captive was when he himself went to the cross. There were a million ways he could've set himself free, but instead . . .

Instead, he took my place so that I could be free. I don't deserve it; but you pardoned me anyway. Outrageous love took my place and fulfilled my sentence. You modeled it so that I could mimic it.

So I release the chains of every negative emotion that has kept me in solitary confinement, right in the middle of everything. I hand them to Jesus, and know he will meet them with love and compassion in his eyes. And I will do the same as I walk out of the darkness into his marvelous light. I'm FREE!!!

God's Word

"Be angry and do not sin; do not let the sun
go down on your anger,
and give no opportunity to the devil."
—Ephesians 4:26–27 ESV

"The Spirit of the Lord GOD is upon me,
because the LORD has anointed me to bring good
news to the poor; he has sent me to bind up the
brokenhearted, to proclaim liberty to the captives, and
the opening of the prison to those who are bound."
—Isaiah 61:1 ESV

"For this reason the Father loves me, because
I lay down my life that I may take it up again.
No one takes it from me, but I lay it down
of my own accord. I have authority to lay it down,
and I have authority to take it up again.
This charge I have received from my Father."
—John 10:17-18 ESV

I'M READY FOR A CHANGE

Hi God. It's time, God. We need to shake things up around here. I need a next-level life, better relationships . . . and let's go up in housing. I'm ready for a promotion. I'm prepared to handle more. Let's *"level up!"* I'm ready for a change!

I want to change everything! The thing about everything changing is, EVERYTHING has to change. If nothing changes . . . nothing changes. I guess that means the first things that have to change are on the inside of me.

Better thinking. Walking in more faith. Breaking those bad habits, like talking down to other people and letting aggravation and doubt creep in (I think you've actually been talking to me about this stuff).

I think you've even been nudging me in some places I'm not comfortable. It's like you want me to give a few things up. But more is more. Less isn't more, is it? Now I'm questioning. I guess, to get more from you, I have to start trusting you more, especially when it looks hard. Geez! Change might be a big deal.

I can't keep trying to change locations, houses, jobs, and friends, hoping that it's going to change me. I can't make an external change and hope for an internal difference. You know that an internal change will result in an external difference. Even better . . . an ETERNAL difference. I have to let you make the changes that you want.

But the things you want are scary. Let go. Let God. Step back. Prefer them. Give it away. Love them, anyway. Could this really be the way UP? I might get so busy taking you literally, at the beginning of transformation, that I MISS what you're trying to do. The end looks so different than the beginning. The two look nothing alike.

A seed looks nothing like an oak tree. A sperm looks nothing like a child. A pile of lumber looks nothing like a home. And my life, up until now, looks nothing like the greatness that the God of Heaven and Earth has planned for me (no matter how great it's been up until now). I'm going to trust you with change.

If it doesn't challenge me, it won't change me. You're giving me the opportunity to take the best part. Why would I turn it down to stay here?

I'm ready for change, God. Bring it on!

God's Word

"Simon Peter said, 'You're the Christ, the Messiah, the Son of the living God.' Jesus came back, 'God bless you, Simon, son of Jonah! You didn't get that answer out of books or from teachers. My Father in heaven, God himself, let you in on this secret of who I really am. And now I'm going to tell you who you are, really are. You are Peter, a rock. This is the rock on which I will put together my church, a church so expansive with energy that not even the gates of hell will be able to keep it out.'"
—Matthew 16:16-18 MSG

"Don't copy the behavior and customs of this world, but let God transform you into a new person by changing the way you think. Then you will learn to know God's will for you, which is good and pleasing and perfect."
—Romans 12:2 NLT

"But our citizenship is in heaven. And we eagerly await a Savior from there, the Lord Jesus Christ, who, by the power that enables him to bring everything under his control, will transform our lowly bodies so that they will be like his glorious body."
—Philippians 3:20-21 NIV

DO I HAVE A DIRTY MIND?

Hi God. My heart gets impure, in the same way my hands get dirty. When I'm shopping in the grocery store, I try not to touch anything nasty. But still, I don't want to lick my fingers. *Gaaarrrrooooosssss*!!!

Unintentional and unavoidable contact with the world causes me to be exposed to everything that's there. Just like viruses and germs in the grocery store are now on me, so are images that flash on the TV, as well as other people's hateful thoughts, offenses, and anger.

I'm infected by music that's piped into stores and conversations that I can't help but overhear. When I spend time with people who don't know you well, they start spouting off doubt and unbelief. Then, my mind, heart, and spirit are covered with the same type of filth!

NASTY. I've got a dirty mind!

My exposure to the world desperately needs to be offset with exposure to your Word. Otherwise, I end up being *double-minded:* half-believing you and thinking like you, and half talking like, walking like, acting like, and thinking like all of the ridiculous mess I've been exposed to! I don't want to have *stinkin' thinkin'!* I want to be in my right mind!

Noooooo! Double-minded, half-committed, a little confused, and back-and-forth makes me unstable in my faith in you, and reaps me a big fat nada, nothing, ZIP! I can't afford that. Wrong thinking leads to wrong living. Who wants that? I need to get in my right mind!

I'm starting a soul-cleansing project! How? Putting more of what you say in me than what they say. If my answer is, "I don't know," I need to research your Word until I DO know, and then repeat that over and over.

I can't let those dust-mongers try to make me like them! I don't want what they have. I don't want to act like they act. And I SURE don't want my attitude to stink like theirs!

I'm spring cleaning my thoughts. I'll deep clean what's coming out of my mouth. And I'm going to RENEW my mind with your Word and align it with the Mind of Christ!

I want what he has, and a dirty mind doesn't get that. It's clean up time! I'm getting my mind right! Right thinking leads to right living! Better than that, God thinking leads to God living. I'm on my way to living your kind of life!

God's Word

"But let him ask in faith, with no doubting,
for he who doubts is like a wave of the sea driven
and tossed by the wind. For let not that man
suppose that he will receive anything from the Lord;
he is a double-minded man, unstable in all his ways."
—James 1:6-8 NKJV

"Come near to God and he will come near to you.
Wash your hands, you sinners, and purify
your hearts, you double-minded."
—James 4:8 NIV

"For 'who has known the mind of the Lord
that he may instruct Him?'
But we have the mind of Christ."
—1 Corinthians 2:16 NKJV

THE ANSWER MAN

Hi God. Sometimes, I smirk when I see all the stupidity happening that I could make better. I mean, the answer is RIGHT THERE! I love it when I'm talking to somebody and I know how to help them get where they want to go. It's exhilarating, walking into something that's limping along and knowing what to do to help. I love making things better. I love being the one with all the answers.

I get into my problem-solving mode. *Let's make it go! Let's help! Let's take this up a notch! All we have to do is . . .* I do that with my own life a lot, too. That switch just flips, and I start moving and adjusting things because I can see where they need to go. I don't even know I'm doing it . . . until it doesn't work.

What's going on here? What in the world? Until now, every time, 2+2=4. How? Huh? I forget that *all I can see is what I can see.* And my *"I-know-what-to-do-here"* mode won't work, in the natural long-term. I need your "God-knows-what-to-do-here" mode.

I don't even realize that I'm in the middle of a mess that I've helped to create until I'm frustrated and confused and can't figure it out. Then, I FINALLY stop and pray. Why does it take me so long?

Why God? Why don't I just get you involved on the very front end? You're the real answer man, not me. I can't care for people. That's your job. You care for them, and I'm just your hands and feet to love them. The care is yours. The concern is yours. The problem is yours. The solution is yours.

I can't even keep my world uncomplicated without you. Fix other people's problems? How, when I have a personal fix-it list a mile long?

My job isn't to get up and go to work making it all good again. You want a relationship, and out of that will come results. I seek you and you show me the way. I don't seek the way and find you as a by-product. My process has been out of order.

I'm passing the baton, Lord. I give you the room you need to handle it your way. The RIGHT way! Your answer is the answer I have needed. Lead me, God. When I follow you, I waste no time. Instruct me. Teach me. I'm ready to act at your command!

God's Word

"I will instruct you and teach you in the way you should go; I will counsel you with my eye upon you."
—Psalm 32:8 ESV

"Surrender your anxiety! Be silent and stop your striving and you will see that I am God. I am the God above all the nations, and I will be exalted throughout the whole earth."
—Psalm 46:10 TPT

"Cast all your anxiety on him because he cares for you."
—1 Peter 5:7 NIV

THE POWER POSITION

Hi God. I was thinking . . . I sure would like it if you would give me a lift. Just a little boost. You know, let me get that promotion I've been working for. I'd love to be the boss for a little bit. Or maybe, give me some awesome ideas so I really shine out in a meeting. Then the boss, and everyone else, would have to listen. I would love to have some people cheer for me, for a minute!

Everybody needs to be in charge, sometimes. A little power never hurt anybody. Put me in charge! I'm READY!

The problem is, power positions in the Spirit and power positions in the flesh look very different. I want to go up and get some long-overdue recognition. And it seems like you're wanting me to humble myself and help somebody else do the exact same thing I'm wanting to do! Um . . . get thee behind me Satan?

Why help them? They're not even nice! They sure don't love you like I do! Wow! Not every position you ask me to take is going to make my flesh happy. If they do, they probably aren't from you. I have to submit to people I don't want to submit to. Do things I don't want to do.

This is frustrating to me! Look, God, isn't it my turn, yet?! I can be *put out* at God, or I can be *put up* by

God. I have to get my soul under control. The more frustrated I get with you for not being raised up . . . the longer it takes. I have to trust you. And trust isn't trusting until it looks completely wrong, and we do it anyway.

It's doing the things that look so beneath my position. But, to honor you and to meet the people you have for me, I have to take my position. I have to operate in your power, not mine. I might not like this, but if I don't take my position, I'll end up in a fetal position. And *ain't nobody got time for that!*

It's not the position that brings the power. It's submitting to your position for me that allows your power to flow through me. The way up isn't up . . . it's DOWN!

Forgive me, Lord, for trying to get something I haven't qualified for yet. I was heading in the wrong direction. Today, I do it your way. I lean into you and your commands. You never disappoint!

"Humble yourselves, therefore, under God's mighty hand, that he may lift you up in due time. Cast all your anxiety on him because he cares for you."
—1 Peter 5:6-7 NIV

"All who lift themselves up will be brought low, and those who make themselves low will be lifted up."
—Luke 14:11 CEB

"He has shown you, O mortal, what is good. And what does the Lord require of you? To act justly and to love mercy and to walk humbly with your God."
—Micah 6:8 NIV

"But he gives more grace. Therefore it says, 'God opposes the proud but gives grace to the humble.'"
—James 4:6 ESV

THE DESERT DRIVE

Hi God. I'm not sure when life took this turn into what seems to look like the Sahara Desert . . . but I don't think I like it!

It seems like, just a few miles back, the view looked just great and everything was on track. I thought I was on track. It seemed like I was connected to Heaven's GPS. I could've sworn I was reading the signs right.

And yet . . .

Things seemed to have dried up out of nowhere. The landscape of life changed. Where I thought things were green and abundant, now . . .not so much. Nothing seems to be growing, no matter what I plant. I'm starting to sweat. I think it's the heat. And it feels like I just need to duck under somewhere to hide and get some relief.

I can't always take things at first glance. Especially at a human, natural glance.

The shortest distance between two points is a straight line. But you aren't interested in *quick*. You want it right. Developed. Full. Ready. BEST!

I have to be ready for you to lead me through something that might resemble a dry place. I have to trust that I'm just transitioning through to the place you have for me.

Sometimes, the long way is actually the shortest way. With you, it's never for less. It's always for more!

What looks like a sun-scorched land may be a shortcut to your best. Just because the view on the journey isn't great it doesn't mean the destination isn't fantastic and sooooo worth it!

Even in the desert land, you take care of your children. The Israelites were there for forty years and never had a need. You led them every step of the way. Hagar was only there for a moment, and you still met her there and sent a spring of water, life, and provision.

You meet me here, a place that looks like no one would want to visit. This territory is familiar to you, and you are here to take me through to the other side. To guide me. To show me the best path. You know where the water holes are. And if there are none, you'll make a new spring of provision, just for me!

I got a little nervous when the scenery first changed. But now, I realize this is my chance to prove to you that I'm not easily shaken. I'm keeping my eyes and ears on your leading, and I'm ready to testify of your goodness in this place!

God's Word

"And the Lord will guide you continually and satisfy your desire in scorched places and make your bones strong; and you shall be like a watered garden, like a spring of water, whose waters do not fail."
—Isaiah 58:11 ESV

"You in your amazing compassion didn't walk off and leave them in the desert. The Pillar of Cloud didn't leave them; daily it continued to show them their route; The Pillar of Fire did the same by night, showed them the right way to go."
—Nehemiah 9:19 MSG

"For 40 years you took good care of them in the desert. They had everything they needed.
Their clothes didn't wear out.
And their feet didn't swell up."
—Nehemiah 9:21 NIRV

I'VE ALWAYS WANTED
A BEST FRIEND

Hi God. I find myself telling people how good you are, and that they should pray to and ask you for things. I get really excited for them. I can sit there and envision you doing something wild for them.

Then, when it comes to *my* prayer time, suddenly, I get a little . . .tense. I hate to say RIGID, but I definitely don't start gushing every thought, dream, and desire to you.

I can't imagine how that must hurt your feelings! You love me more than anything! You knew what I was going to do wrong before you decided to create me. You knew I would let you down. You knew I would fall. You knew I would fail. You knew I would get mad. You KNEW!

And yet . . .

Your love never changed. Only my perception of it changed.

I started hiding things from you so that . . .what . . .you wouldn't find out? You already know! All you want is an intimacy with me: for me to trust you with things that I would hesitate to tell my best friend—

things you already know, but want me to confide in you anyway.

You've never given up my secrets. It doesn't even occur to you to kick me when I'm down. You're the *lifter of my head.* When I count myself out, you smile, pick me up, and whisper in my ear, "My child, not your strength. Mine. Lean into me. I'm here. I've always been here. Let me carry the weight!"

WHY??? Why haven't I believed that you would be so good to me? Why wouldn't I give you the chance to blow me away? Why won't I dare to accept that you are not only a gracious and loving God, but You are also my Father? My Daddy. My caretaker. My cheerleader. My BEST FRIEND!

A best friend that will never rat me out, try to trade up for someone more popular, or get too busy for me.

I've needed you my entire life! You've been here alllll along, waiting for me to wake up to your sweet gift of friendship and confidence.

Now that we're here, I'm ready to open up to you. I'm going to step out and tell you all of my secrets. I'm willing to trust you with the hidden things that I've been too scared to tell anyone . . . maybe even myself.

I've been looking for a friend like you my whole life!

God's Word

"Before I formed you in the womb I knew you;
Before you were born I sanctified you; I ordained
you a prophet to the nations."
—Jeremiah 1:5 NKJV

"But You, O LORD, *are* a shield for me, My glory
and the One who lifts up my head."
—Psalm 3:3 NKJV

"Greater love has no one than this: to lay down one's
life for one's friends. You are my friends if
you do what I command. I no longer call you servants,
because a servant does not know his master's business.
Instead, I have called you friends, for everything that
I learned from my Father I have made known to you."
—John 15:13-15 NIV

STOPPING SHORT

Hi God. Sometimes, I stop looking just when something comes along that could be my answer. I need to lift up my eyes and look further.

Why do I stop close to the answer?

Why do I stop short of where I know in my soul that I'm supposed to go?

Why do I stop when things cease to be convenient? "After all," I think, "This is close enough, right?"

Here's the problem with that: When I don't go all the way to where I feel you, in my spirit, pushing me to go, I stop short of the *best* that you have for me.

I can only see so far when I'm standing on the ground. If I was standing on a skyscraper, I could see much further. The horizon would open up, and I could really get a grasp on what was happening. But exactly what could I see? *Further*, for sure . . . but not far enough!

The most incredible natural wisdom in the world doesn't hold a candle to what you know, God. You are the beginning. You made everything I see. You started it and manufactured it. You wrote the end from the beginning!

Since I'm still having to deal with natural circumstances, so many things block my view. It all depends on which way I look and what's happening that day—clouds (of doubt), the fog (of uncertainty), the storms (of life), and obstacles as big a buildings that no one can argue with. It affects what I can see.

When I'm on an airplane, I can see so much more! The higher I go, the more I can see. But even at 40,000 feet, I only get a tiny glimpse of what you can see, God.

Why don't I ask you what *you* can see, God? You're calling me up higher. You're calling me to see how you see . . . to look with eyes of faith.

You see my entire future—the path you've set before me. You see the possibilities I'll have if I'll follow your leading. You see with eyes of hope. You see exactly what you've called me to. You see the blessing that you have for me. You see the level you've created me to reach. You see the importance of me trusting what you see, and You're trying to help me see it.

I won't stop short of my purpose just because I can't see what you can. I will lift my eyes. I will look to you to guide me with what *you* see, Lord.

God's Word

"'For my thoughts are not your thoughts,
neither are your ways my ways,' declares the Lord.
'As the heavens are higher than the earth, so are
my ways higher than your ways and my thoughts
than your thoughts.'"
—Isaiah 55:8-9 NIV

"For we live by faith, not by sight."
—2 Corinthians 5:7 NIV

"Lift up your eyes on high and see: who created these?
He who brings out their host by number, calling them
all by name; by the greatness of his might and because
he is strong in power, not one is missing."
—Isaiah 40:26 ESV

I NEED A
MOMMA BEAR

Hi God. Have you noticed how momma bears are protective of their cubs? You might mess with the momma bear, but ain't NOBODY gonna mess with the baby! They might swat their cubs from time to time, to keep them out of trouble. But they're blameless because they would lay down their life for them.

I've even seen it with the most loving of parents. I don't question when a momma or poppa guides and corrects a little one. I can easily see the commitment, and their depth of unconditional love, no matter how frustrated they get.

Still, these model parents' love pales in comparison to your love for me, God. Unconditional, non-refundable, non-exchangeable, you-got- it-now-you're-stuck-with-it love, protection, AND correction.

A real parent's love doesn't come without protection and correction – even if that parent is a bear and not a human. So why, God, would I possibly think that your love would leave me exposed?

Why would I think your course correction and sharing with me—what to do, and what not to do—would be anything but the most precious love? Why would I resist your instructions? What have you ever done to hurt me? And how much have you given to protect me?

No caring parent is all "yes" and never "no." Your "no" is your protection, keeping me from getting what I want but not wanting what I get. I need your spiritual eyes to discern what I can't see.

Your protection is you whispering in my ear which way to go, which deal to take, and which relationship to avoid. You know the end from the beginning. That kind of knowledge of the future is priceless!

Your protection sometimes feels like a despised denial, in the moment. But it's actually a precious cushion, keeping me from harm that I don't even know about. You protect me even when I resist you. I can't thank you enough for never giving up on me!

You are the most courageous, loving, protective *momma-bear-of-a-God* I could ever hope or pray for. Thank you for loving me big enough to protect me from myself and every other thing the enemy uses to try to derail me from the exciting future you have for me!

God's Word

"(Love) always protects, always trusts,
always hopes, always perseveres."
—1 Corinthians 13:7 NIV

"For the LORD corrects those he loves, just as
a father corrects a child in whom he delights."
—Proverbs 3:12 NLT

"I give them eternal life, and they shall never
perish; no one will snatch them out of my hand.
My Father, who has given them to me, is greater
than all; no one can snatch them out of my Father's
hand. I and the Father are one."
—John 10:28-30 NIV

"Whoever dwells in the shelter of the Most High
will rest in the shadow of the Almighty. I will say
of the LORD, "He is my refuge and my fortress,
my God, in whom I trust."
—Psalm 91:1-2 NIV

IT'S SO TIGHT

Hi God. I feel like I'm inching along one step at a time. They're not even big steps. There's no running, no leaps, no bounds. Just inch. Stop. Inch. Stop. INCH.

Sometimes, it seems like I'm the only one still down here crawling around. How *did* everybody else get way up there??? And then, it seems to get worse!

I get all wrapped up in trying to make things happen. Money gets tight. Time gets even tighter. I begin to feel like there's nowhere to turn. The more I struggle, the more constricted I feel. It's like I'm so wrapped up that I almost can't move . . . and it all goes dark.

But then . . .

There's something on the inside. Like something I didn't even know existed within me has suddenly come to life. This Life brings a will to fight—to believe—to break out of this mess. As I become willing to gnaw away at the anger, hurt, and bitterness that have brought me here, I sense that something is changing.

Then, I wish someone from the outside would help. I know I got myself into this . . .but can't *anybody* see me trying to get out?

But no one comes to help. It's just me, and this Life inside me, working our way out. I'm too busy working my way out to notice that this fight is giving me strength. What is this strength? Where did it come from? Oh . . .it's You, God.

Then, almost unexpectedly, freedom comes. And not only freedom but wings to fly.

The chains that were meant to bind me are gone: You used them as a cocoon to help me gain the strength to fly. I didn't know I was a caterpillar. I didn't realize You were using my apparent bondage as a cocoon. I couldn't see all that You had planned.

But now, this I know: Your plans for me include wings to fly to places higher than I ever imagined. You are with me in the dark places, and You will never leave me there.

Come out, butterfly! Your time has come!

God's Word

"I'll show up and take care of you as I promised and bring you back home. I know what I'm doing. I have it all planned out—plans to take care of you, not abandon you, plans to give you the future you hope for."
—Jeremiah 29:11 MSG

"And we know that in all things God works for the good of those who love him, who have been called according to his purpose."
—Romans 8:28 NIV

"I will walk about in freedom, for I have sought out your precepts."
—Psalm 119:45 NIV

JUGGLING ACT

Hi God. As I think about what daily life requires—juggling schedules, responsibilities, priorities, time with you, time for me (does that even exist?), and time for family and friends—I know that my coordination skills will be tested.

Just when I think I have everything balanced and flowing smoothly, here comes some big heavy thing that's way out of balance. Then . . . KABOOM! Everything comes crashing to the floor. But I can't stop! I don't think I can relax, because I don't think that there's time for that.

God, you know what's coming my way, today. And you're ready to help me through it!

My days aren't well planned, right on time, and flawlessly executed, because life throws unexpected curve balls at me, daily! Maybe I've been trying to juggle too much for too long. Every once in a while, I get tired and take my eye off the ball. Then there are times when some wise guy will throw something into the mix . . . something I wasn't expecting.

I keep thinking I've got to pick up everything, clean up the mess as quickly as possible, and get my life going again. After all, someone is depending on me. If the juggler quit the circus every time she dropped the ball . . . she'd be in for a very short career.

I guess the truth of the matter is, without taking some time to think—to put myself together, to rest, to let my stress levels recede back to a non-emergency level – none of those people or things are going to get the best of me anyway.

Of course, I'll occasionally drop the ball. But you say not to lose heart! I know you're ready to help me through it. Even if I fall, you're already there to pull me back up. You pick up my problems and my stresses and carry them for me. I know your yoke is easy, and your burden is light. I will carry yours, so you can carry mine!

I trust you will help me prioritize my life and remove the juggling acts I don't need to be carrying. I'll spend the next few days working on making sure I take care of me so that I can take care of others. Thank you for helping me relax in your presence.

God's Word

"Give your burdens to the Lord and he will take care of you. He will not permit the godly to slip and fall."
—Psalm 55:22 NLT

"Therefore we do not lose heart. Though outwardly we are wasting away, yet inwardly we are being renewed day by day."
—2 Corinthians 4:16 NIV

"Fear not, for I am with you; be not dismayed, for I am your God; I will strengthen you, I will help you, I will uphold you with my righteous right hand."
—Isaiah 41:10 ESV

THE FIXER

Hi God. I hate when I see messed up things that could easily be fixed! A couple minutes' time, an easy solution, a quick change, a new idea, a little system – tiny things can make a big difference.

I see easily fixable things everywhere. "Why doesn't she just . . .." "An easy answer for that would be . . ." "That wouldn't happen anymore if only . . ." Sometimes, I think it's such a gift to think like this. Other times, it drives me crazy!

I'm trying to fix every messed up thing in my day, week, schedule, house – *life*! It's overwhelming! I can see what things are *supposed* to be like, but actually getting them that way . . . *ugh*!

To be honest, I don't pray about most of these things. When I think I know what to do, I just do it on autopilot. It's as natural as knowing to turn the water off after you wash your hands. I guess the real issue is that I *think* I know what to do. But I don't know what *you* want me to do.

What you want to happen and what I'm trying to make happen, don't always add up. And when I'm trying to make things happen, I'm relying on me – not you. That gets super overwhelming and makes my head spin. My frustration rises, and I start to feel like a failure!

There isn't anywhere in the Bible that says, "Go ye into the world and take on all their cares and fix all their problems." I guess I started re-writing Heaven's policies. You want me to come to you and lay the problem at your feet.

When I talk to you about it, I begin to get Heaven's perspective. From way up there, the things that look huge and monumental start to take on an eternal viewpoint and become easy to handle.

I have to learn a new process: See something that needs to be fixed. Pause. Pray. Listen and lean into your ability . . . not mine!

It feels like 10,000 pounds just came off of my shoulders! I'm not responsible for making all this happen. I don't have what it takes. But you do!

Thank you, Father, for being with me every step of the way, and being the ultimate "Fixer."

"Blessed are those who have learned to acclaim you,
who walk in the light of your presence, O Lord."
—Psalm 89:15 NIV

"I have told you these things, so that in me you may
have peace. In this world you will have trouble.
But take heart! I have overcome the world."
—John 16:33 NIV

"The LORD is good to those who wait for him,
a refuge on the day of distress, taking care of those
who look to him for protection."
—Nahum 1:7-8 NABRE

CAN YOU HEAR ME NOW?

Hi God. When I call out your name, sometimes I look up to the sky, and it seems like heaven is so eternally far away. Can you even hear me from here? Hello? Can you hear me now?

I forget that, whenever I say the name "Jesus," all Heaven and Earth can hear. Not only Heaven and Earth but also the enemy. Your name is a local call. Your name transcends every realm. Your name is all-powerful. The name of Jesus is the Name above every name that has existed or will ever exist.

No matter where I am – even if I'm somewhere I know I'm not supposed to be – the name of Jesus is still a local call from there, and brings with it all POWER!

When I utter that name, every knee will bow. When I say that name, all realms take note. When I proclaim that name, it shakes everything up and starts setting it in Heavenly order. When I declare your name, it invokes your promise.

There is no more powerful word, phrase, or sentence in all the universe than the name of JESUS! And you've given me the authority to use your name! What trust you put in me, Lord!

Why was I nervous that you couldn't hear me from here? Why was I concerned that our reception might be bad? You have put the power of your Word and your name in my mouth!

I'm not scared of proximity or clarity of call, anymore! I'm going to start dropping the Name on it! Jesus, Jesus, JESUS! In the name of Jesus, by the blood of Jesus!

Salvation comes with your name! Healing happens at your name. I am justified in your name. The enemy has no power against your name. Everything I do is in your name!

Thank you, Lord, for the availability, trust, ability, and power to proclaim and pray in your name!

God's Word

"Therefore God also has highly exalted Him
and given Him the name which is above every name,
that at the name of Jesus every knee should bow,
of those in heaven, and of those on earth,
and of those under the earth."
—Philippians 2:9-10 NKJV

"When the seventy-two disciples returned,
they joyfully reported to him, 'Lord, even the demons
obey us when we use your name!'"
—Luke 10:17 NLT

'For 'whoever calls on the name of the Lord
shall be saved.'"
—Romans 10:13 NKJV

"And such were some of you. But you were washed,
you were sanctified, you were justified in the name of
the Lord Jesus Christ and by the Spirit of our God."
—1 Corinthians 6:11 ESV

A NEEDED RUBBERNECK

Hi God. How many situations have I been delivered from, gotten out of, or received a miracle in . . . only for me to credit coincidence with my miracle? Or even worse, for me not to notice what you did for me at all?

My headache went away, and I talked about how the Ibuprofen finally took effect. I had a cold for one day instead of a week, and I bragged about my immune system. The money I needed came in, and I said, "About time!" The kids calmed down, and I was too busy not losing my mind to even consider how it happened. The boss changed his mind about all the nonsense he was saying, and I just thought he finally became sane – *or not!* (Lol.)

You like doing things for me. You revel in defeating the enemy for me and allowing me to have the victory. You've told me in your Word that you are Provider, Deliverer, Redeemer, Healer . . . and so much more.

All you want from me is the recognition that it was YOU, and not me. It was your miracle-working power, not happenstance. It was your divine timing, not coinkydink. It was your healing power, not a misdiagnosis.

I pray and hope for minutes, days, weeks - wait, MONTHS— for some things. And then, to treat it like a passing road sign on the highway of life . . .? Why would I give an accident on the highway a second look, but plow forward with eyes glued to the road when it comes to you?

I've gotten mad at "rubberneck" drivers for slowing down before, but that's exactly what I need to do. I need to slow down and take a second look at all you've done for me.

You told the Israelites to build a memorial so they'd never forgot how unbelievably good you were to them. You know my human tendency is to move right along. I won't do that now, Lord.

You'll use my miracle to prove to other people how great you are. You'll draw people to yourself by your goodness if I'll just tell of it. And I will. I'll stop, look, and tell, tell, tell of your greatness!

Taking my time to "rubberneck," and look at how mind-blowingly phenomenal you've been to me, is one of the best things I can ever do!

"Come and see what God has done,
his awesome deeds for mankind!"
—Psalm 66:5 NIV

"I am doing this so all who see this miracle
will understand what it means—
that it is the Lord who has done this, the Holy One
of Israel who created it."
—Isaiah 41:20 NLT

"I will remember the deeds of the Lord;
yes, I will remember your miracles of long ago."
—Psalm 77:11 NIV

DREAMS

Hi God. Sometimes, I get really excited about the dreams you've put in my heart. It's almost like I can close my eyes and see those crazy places with such clarity that I think they're real! That is, until something snaps me back to right now. It's like I live in an alternate reality.

However, I'm learning that I can't tell my dreams to just anyone. Not everybody sees in me what you do. And holy cow, they don't mind letting me *know* it! I mean, seriously?

It's not just that I feel unsupported—it's like these people seem determined to *kill* my dream and maybe even take *me* down in the process! Why? Why are they so threatened by the dream in my heart?

You've planted such . . .*desire* in me! And they have planted such . . .*doubts*!

I have to remember that, when you ordain my future, no other human can change it. Only *I* can allow my dream to die. With you on my side, that's not going to happen! Not today, Satan!

No matter what they say about me—regardless of whether or not people believe in me—there is a God who believes in me! You created me for a purpose. You didn't need just another body—you wanted *me*! You intentionally pursue me; you crafted me with a specific plan in mind: a dream that's not just mine, but yours! And you want to bring it to pass through ME!

Because of you, I can believe in myself, even when no one else does.

You wouldn't have given me this dream unless you already had a way to bring it to pass! I'm not trying to make something happen. I simply need to follow the preordained footsteps you've laid out for me!

So many people want the dream without the journey. They want the finish line without the race; the promise but not the process. That's not going to be my attitude. I'm willing to take it all!

You're a God who turns "can't" into "can" and dreams into plans! Regardless of trouble, stress, haters, or mess, you're making a way for my dream!

My desires aren't just whimsical fantasies; you gave me these desires so you could fulfill them! I'm honored to be dreaming with you. I'm ready to live out the dreams, plans, and purposes that you have for me.

God's Word

"Delight yourself in the Lord, and he will give you the desires of your heart."
—Psalms 37:4 ESV

"I knew you before I formed you in your mother's womb. Before you were born I set you apart and appointed you as my prophet to the nations."
—Jeremiah 1:5 NLT

"The steps of a [good and righteous] man are directed and established by the Lord, and He delights in his way [and blesses his path]."
—Psalms 37:23 AMP

I FEEL LOST

Hi God. Where am I? I'm in the middle of everything, doing the best I can to keep up with it all, and somehow, I feel like I'm going nowhere. I stay up later, work harder, give it my all, and fall into bed feeling like I'm just spinning my wheels. I've gone nowhere: I'm lost!

The song "Amazing Grace" jumps into my head whenever I say that. "I once was lost . . ." That's me. I need you to find me! Find me, and show me where I go from here. Why can't I hear you? Why don't I see what you have for me?

I feel like I'm in the *dark*. Could you shed some light on my path here? You know everything!

I want you to light up what's going on AROUND me. And maybe, you're wanting to shed some light on what's going on IN me.

Your Word says that when I don't walk in love, I'm in the dark. So who am I angry with? Who is driving me nuts? Why am I stepping out of love and getting lost in the dark because of them? Who haven't I forgiven? Who am I blaming for where I am?

If I'm blaming someone for where I am, I should be using that energy to believe you for getting me out of here. Anger, resentment, aggravation, blame, hate—none of that connects me to you. It separates me.

If Jesus hung on the cross and prayed, "Forgive them, for they know not what they do," then I should be able to trust you with what has been done to me . . . and let it go. Not releasing these hurts is anchoring me to this lost place and to this darkness.

Knowledge is power. I can't do this alone, God. But with you, I can do ALL things! Help me to forgive them and walk in your love. You ARE love. Then your light comes on! You light my path.

Not only do you light up where I am and cause things to take shape and become clear; but I can see where you want to take me! I'm not lost anymore! I can see the way you want me to go lit up in front of me!

I'm tired of being lost, Lord! I give it up. I give them up. I'm not holding onto this darkness anymore! I release it! I will love the unlovely. Now, bring in light and direction. Let's get out of here, and on to the great things I know you have planned for me!

"Anyone who says, 'I am in the light' while holding
hatred in his heart toward a fellow believer
is still in the darkness."
—1 John 2:9 TPT

"But whoever hates a fellow believer lives in the
darkness – stumbling around in the dark with no clue
where he is going, for he is blinded by the darkness."
—1 John 2:11 TPT

"Thy word is a lamp unto my feet and a light
unto my path."
—Psalm 119:105 KJV

"If we claim that we share life with him,
but keep walking in the realm of darkness,
we're fooling ourselves and not living the truth.
But if we keep living in the pure light that surrounds
him, we share *unbroken* fellowship with one
another, and the blood of Jesus, his Son,
continually cleanses us from all sin."
—1 John 1:6-7 TPT

COMPLAIN AND REMAIN

Hi God. You're not going to believe the day I had. I mean . . .for real! This is one for the record books: a comedy of errors with incompetence and stupidity *everywhere*!

What? You don't want the details? Huh? "Stop talking?" But I thought you wanted to hear about my challenges!

Oh . . . you want to hear about *real* problems, not just me complaining? Oooohhhh . . .I guess there *is* a difference.

The Israelites did it. They complained about your miracle manna from heaven and wanted meat instead. They saw you astoundingly part the Red Sea and a measly three days later, complained and doubted you could even provide water for them. They just saw you do miracles! But I've seen you do a lot for me, too!

That must be how I sound when I'm not thankful— when things don't meet my "standards."

Complain and remain . . .That's what happened to the Israelites for *forty years!* I don't want to be stuck in a holding pattern! I want to *praise* and get a *raise* instead!

If I look at your Word, it tells me to be thankful for everything. What's left? Nothing. If I really think about it . . .*no thing*!

And what do I have to complain about, anyway? You've removed mountains, made the impossible possible, moved heaven and earth, sent Jesus to die for me, and extended more mercy and grace to me than I could ever use!

If I can't see you working for me, it simply means I'm *blind* to exactly how good you are. You've saved me from more than I can even conceive.

I started out complaining; and now, I want to apologize!

When I make the choice to thank you, in faith, for the circumstances I don't like - that's my faith in action! Faith pleases you. Complaining does not. I can't blame you, Father. When people complain to me, it annoys me, too!

So, instead of bending your ear about some trivial nonsense, I'll trust that whatever garbage I'm complaining about was actually a whole lot better than whatever hell and heartache you saved me from. I'm blissfully unaware, and I'm just going to say, *thank you*!

Thank you, for being patient with me. Thank you, for loving me even when I can be irritating. Thank you, for teaching me. Thank you, for accepting me right where I am and loving me too much to leave me here.

You're *so* good to me, God! You made today just for me. And guess what? I'm going to go and enjoy it!

"In everything give thanks; for this is the will
of God in Christ Jesus for you."
—1 Thessalonians 5:18 NKJV

"Nor complain, as some of them also complained,
and were destroyed by the destroyer."
—1 Corinthians 10:10 NKJV

This is the day the LORD has made;
We will rejoice and be glad in it.
—Psalm 118:24 NKJV

DOES ANYBODY
EVEN SEE ME?

Hi God. I mean, if you're even there. Does anybody even care? Can anybody even see me over here? I feel like I'm screaming for help and waving my arms back and forth, but nobody even slows down to look. It's like I'm . . . INVISIBLE.

I don't think anyone sees where I am . . . but you see everything!

You saw when Hagar was forced to have the child of a man who would never love her. She ran away into the desert. But you didn't leave her to die. You sent one of your angels to meet her there. She knew there was no way anyone could have found her. She gave you a new name: You-Are-The-God-Who-Sees.

When shepherd boy, David, seemingly forgotten, ignored, and passed over, was on the back of an obscure hill and all his brothers were lined up to be the next king – you saw him. You weren't going to let that promotion happen without your man on the scene. David was unseen by human eyes but seen in the Spirit. You are the God who sees!

When Hannah was barren, heartbroken, and crushed, her cries didn't fall on deaf ears. You heard her wail your name. You saw every tear. And your patience wasn't callous; it was predetermined. You needed a prophet named Samuel to be born at a specific time so that he could speak for you on the Earth.

It's not that you didn't see her. It wasn't unsympathetic ignorance. It was your significant timing. You are the God who sees.

Maybe that's what it is with me!

I want you to get to work, right now, in a way that I can see you moving. But you would rather hold my miracle for the moment that will bring the most impact.

More glory for you, more goodness for me. You aren't nearsighted. I'm not wearing unintentional camouflage. Your eyes have been going back and forth, over all the Earth, lining things up. Your vision is good and your eyes are fixed on me. Your plan is exceptional, and your timing is intentional.

I've been waiting for someone to notice. You've been covering me so I don't move too early and miss all of the blessings you've been putting together for me.

Okay, God—I see you! I see you seeing me. We're making eye-to-eye contact. I call you *"You-Are-the-God-Who-Sees"* and I'm going through my day in peace. I trust you!

God's Word

"Then she made a vow and said, 'O LORD of hosts, if You will indeed look on the affliction of Your maidservant and remember me, and not forget Your maidservant, but will give Your maidservant a male child, then I will give him to the LORD all the days of his life, and no razor shall come upon his head.'"
—1 Samuel 1:11 NKJV

"Then Eli answered and said, 'Go in peace, and the God of Israel grant your petition which you have asked of Him.'"
—1 Samuel 1:17 NKJV

"And Samuel said to Jesse, 'Are all the young men here?' Then he said, 'There remains yet the youngest, and there he is, keeping the sheep.' And Samuel said to Jesse, 'Send and bring him. For we will not sit down till he comes here.'"
—1 Samuel 16:11 NKJV

"For the eyes of the LORD run to and fro throughout the whole earth, to show Himself strong on behalf of *those* whose heart *is* loyal to Him.
—2 Chronicles 16:9 KJV

AN UNWANTED ANCHOR

Hi God. I keep jumping after sparkles in the air. But I'm just jumping up and down . . . not rising. I keep falling back to the ground. It's like there's an anchor tied to me that I can't see. It only lets me go so far, then . . .BAM! It pulls me right back down!

You say that you want to bring something new in me, even if I can't see it. You want me to rise on wings, like an EAGLE!

But an eagle doesn't wear a leash on its leg. You see what's holding me down. You know the part of me that keeps holding me back. After all, you're not the one holding me back. You want my freedom as much as I do!

You see my pride – unwillingness – rebellion – stubbornness – selfishness – the way that I chase money instead of chasing majesty— the way I start craving the spotlight instead of your Spirit.

You open the cage. You have broken the bonds that tether me.

But I still have to commit to leaving the familiar. But I've never had such a nice cage—I mean house.

I've never gotten so much prestige or attention – it's what's holding me here.

My previous success, in the flesh, is what's holding me here. I have to let go, not only be cut free. I have to trust you in what you're calling me to, instead of leaning into what I can do on my own.

What if the best things about my life are the very reasons I don't soar to the heights that I really want?

What if I'm holding on to what I have and those things are anchoring me to where I am, right now?

There are some new places you're calling me to go that are exactly where I am . . . only higher: the same work, but with the purpose and fulfillment, I've always hoped for. The same people, but the closeness I've always ached for. And a love that's so fresh and overwhelming it feels like the first time I walked in. It was new and exciting!

The same life, but an incredible enthusiasm, vigor, and excitement—like it's Christmas!

God, you do a new thing! Don't I see it? Don't I trust you? I do! I do! I DO!

The chains are off, and I won't sink back down into my old mindsets, moods, and attitudes. I'm ready to keep my hands off that anchor and let you help me RISE!

God's Word

"We have escaped like a bird from the fowler's snare;
the snare has been broken, and we have escaped."
—Psalm 124:7 NIV

"But those who wait on the Lord Shall renew
their strength; They shall mount up with wings
like eagles, They shall run and not be weary,
They shall walk and not faint."
—Isaiah 40:31 NKJV

"'It shall come about on that day,' says the Lord
of hosts, 'that I will break the yoke off your neck
and I will tear off your bonds and force apart your
shackles, and strangers will no longer make slaves
of the people [of Israel].'"
—Jeremiah 30:8 AMP

SINGLE AND READY TO MINGLE

Hi God. Here I stand, looking around at all these sappy, in-love, married couples. I didn't have a "plus one" for my invitation. I want my "plus one!" Not just a "plus one" . . . I want the person you made for me. My helpmate. A buddy. A best friend!

I feel like a "half" trying to find the rest of me. I know that isn't true. I know I'm WHOLE and complete in you. And honestly, I know that if I'm looking to any person to give me what you have promised to give me, I either delay *my* blessing or negate it altogether.

There's no person on the planet who can make me feel the love and acceptance that Jesus died to give me. I will keep you first place. And I promise not to get over-excited and get things out of order . . . because then, you won't bless it.

But right now, I feel desolate! On a planet with seven billion people, I don't want to travel this journey alone. That's why you call me "Hephzibah" and you call me "Beulah." God, you call me married. God, you say your delight is in me! It's not me just wishing. You're better than E-Harmony, and you're calling in my spouse!

Just like Abraham charged his servant to bring back a wife for Isaac, you're looking to and fro to connect me with the person you've always known will be my love and my future. I'm not sending a servant from my family. I have you, the God of the Universe, working things out for me!

And in the meantime, I'm not alone. You're my husband and creator. You've promised to take care of me better than any earthly husband or wife. You are my "plus one," until that cute thing you have for me is revealed. I'm not alone. I'm well taken care of on the way to the beautiful person you have for me!

I'm not settling, Lord. I'm going to make sure they love you as much as I do. I'll make sure they love me like I'll love them. And we will serve you TOGETHER!

I trust your timing. If it hasn't worked out - I believe your will is never for less, it's always for more! My prince charming (my princess) is a man (or lady) in waiting, praying for me just like I'm praying for them.

Lord, send them to me and trust me to care for them like you do. Trust me to build them up and be considerate of their feelings, hopes, and dreams. You've taught me what it feels like to be LOVED WELL. I will pour that out on your precious child you trust me with!

God's Word

"You shall also be a crown of glory in the hand of the Lord, and a royal diadem in the hand of your God. You shall no longer be termed forsaken, nor shall your land any more be termed Desolate; but you shall be called Hephzibah, and your land Beulah; for the Lord delights in you, and your land shall be married."
—Isaiah 62:3-4 NKJV

"He who finds a wife finds a good thing and obtains favor from the Lord."
—Proverbs 18:22 ESV

"For your Creator will be your husband; the Lord of Heaven's Armies is his name! He is your Redeemer, the Holy One of Israel, the God of all the earth."
—Isaiah 54:5 NLT

"The LORD God said, 'It is not good for the man to be alone. I will make a helper suitable for him.'"
—Genesis 2:18 NIV

I KNOW ALL ABOUT THAT

Hi God. I hate to admit it, but sometimes I tune people out because I already know what they're going to say. I mean, SERIOUSLY, do they have to share all those details? I could write a book and paint the house before they get finished. #eyeroll. Nobody cares!

It's like when I go to church, and they're talking about a Bible story I've already heard or a verse I've learned. AGAIN? I don't want to cover something I already know and am familiar with. I want something NEW!

But so many of the things that you do look like something we've seen before. It wasn't just another poor baby being born in a bad part of town. It was the Savior of the world entering our realm!

It wasn't just another thief and liar being crucified for their wrongs. It was the separation of Heaven and Earth being torn, and grace flooding into the Earth for us to access.

It wasn't just another cloud in the sky. It was your literal GLORY filling the church and reaching out for Your sweet, loved children.

Just because it might seem like something I've seen before doesn't mean I should treat it as common.

He wasn't JUST a carpenter's son. He was the Word who became flesh and lived among us.

It's not JUST worship. It's an intimate moment when my praise graces the ears of the King.

It's not JUST a prayer. It's an important conversation with the Creator of the Universe.

It's not JUST a Scripture. It's a relevant Word that answers the very questions I'm asking.

It's not JUST a message. It's a divinely-connected revelation to my spirit of your caring for me—an encouragement to my soul.

I have to be willing to look at things that seem familiar to me and try to see what I haven't seen before. Skepticism and doubt will hold me back from the glory, wisdom, power, and blessing you've sent for me.

I'm sorry, God, for making the phenomenal familiar. Forgive me, Lord. I see you. And when I don't see you, I will look for you in the things I'm overlooking because I think I've seen them before.

"Then the cloud covered the tabernacle of meeting, and the glory of the LORD filled the tabernacle. And Moses was not able to enter the tabernacle of meeting, because the cloud rested above it, and the glory of the LORD filled the tabernacle."
—Exodus 40:34-35 NKJV

"And in the morning you will see the glory of the LORD, because he has heard your grumbling against him. Who are we, that you should grumble against us?"
—Exodus 16:7 NIV

"And she brought forth her firstborn Son, and wrapped Him in swaddling cloths, and laid Him in a manger, because there was no room for them in the inn."
—Luke 2:7 NKJV

"And they said, 'Is not this Jesus, the son of Joseph, whose father and mother we know? How is it then that He says, 'I have come down from heaven?'"
—John 6:42 NKJV

PRESSURE

Hi God. There's pressure that comes with new heights. When I start to rise up—when I begin to ascend—I feel that the air is . . .thinner. It's harder to breathe!

More people are counting on me. The work is harder. The spotlight is brighter. The *spiritual* pressure has increased. So I tend to step back; back to the very place I want to leave. It's a place of familiarity and comfort. Except that it isn't comfortable. I don't want to be here! I can hardly catch my breath.

I'm so mad at myself, confused about how I got here and aggravated! It feels like I'm being sabotaged . . . but by whom? Me? You? No: by the enemy. He's using this pressure against me.

I step up, and I know I'm *supposed* to be here. Jesus, you died for my freedom. You've provided me with opportunity. You've gifted me with the skills to be here, even though as I stand in this new place, I'm doubting myself to the core.

Doubt, pressure, a stripping away of confidence – these are all the tools of the enemy to get me to step back and step down. These aren't *real*! They're *shadowy lies* of the enemy—spiritual warfare!

A shadow can't hurt me. I can just walk right through it. You beckon me from the other side, *"Come, my child. Trust me when you feel unworthy."* You call me up. You summon me *through*. My ascent is sure, with you at my side. You are *right here*!

You're cheering for me! You're calling me to soar to new heights. Who will I listen to? Will I let a shadow frighten me, like a child?

Not today, Satan! Your gig is up! I see you lurking! Your creepy, shadowy seeds of doubt are being uprooted, right now. When light enters, shadows flee!

God, I invite you into the middle of this feeling of pressure and insecurity. You're greater than any feeling. I trust you to hold me here when I can't hold myself!

I *will* stay at these new heights! I'm not going back!!!

God's Word

"The Lord is my light and my salvation—
so why should I be afraid? The Lord is my fortress,
protecting me from danger, so why should I tremble?"
—Psalm 27:1 NLT

"Yea, though I walk through the valley of the shadow
of death, I will fear no evil; For You *are* with me;
Your rod and Your staff, they comfort me."
—Psalm 23:4 NKJV

"Little children, you are from God and have
overcome them, for he who is in you is greater
than he who is in the world."
—1 John 4:4 ESV

"So then, surrender to God. Stand up to the
devil and resist him and he will turn and
run away from you."
—James 4:7 TPT

WHAT'S IN A NAME?

Hi God. Let's be honest. Most of the time when we're talking . . . it's about me! The things I'm needing to hear from you about. The direction I need. Getting a word from you. Asking you to move.

But truly, I need to spend more time talking about YOU. Who you are and how good you are. When I get time with you, I need to refocus on exactly WHO I'm talking to. I call you *God*. I pray in the name of *Jesus*. But your name is so much more than that and so descriptive of who you are.

God means love. Your name is *Love*. When I say your name, I'm saying love. You are *King of Kings* and *Lord of Lords*. You are *Majesty*. Robed. Regal. Ceremonial and formal. You are *Father, Abba, Daddy*. The King of the entire universe, but also, a loving and correcting father that welcomes me into his lap. I am the pleasure of your soul!

You are the *God-Who-Sees-Me* where I am, and the *Provider* of all I need, from air to finances and everything in between. Your name is *Healer* of any problem my body ever encounters. You are the *Lover of My Soul*, my *Redeemer*, and my *Righteousness*. All that I can never earn on my own. It's not what you have – it's who you are!

You are the *Bright and Morning Star*. You are *Light* in every situation. And where light IS darkness cannot stay. Your name could be translated *Darkness Destroyer!*

You are the *Lion of the Tribe of Judah*, fierce enough to win any fight. But also, *The Lamb*, gentle and approachable. And at the same time, my *Shepherd* who watches over and protects me. Your name is *Peace*. You are my peace.

You are my *Banner*. Your banner over me is love. You are the provider of my banner year. You are the owner of the cattle on a thousand hills. Actually, you are *Creator*. You created the cattle, and every resource is renewable when it comes to you. You made it in the first place, and can make it again—even if it's a new pancreas or a new heart!

You are the *Alpha and Omega*; the beginning and the end. You are the all-knowing and all-seeing God. Any answer I need, you've had since the beginning of time. You not only are *Wisdom*, you provide it when I ask.

You are *I AM*. Anything I need, you are. Any gap in the world, you are. Anything I need to know, you are. Any time I need, you are.

Your name is *Power!* And at your name, every knee will bow!

Father, God, Saviour, Redeemer, Provider, Creator, Healer, Peace-Giver, Seer, Protector, Banner, Peace, Love . . .and so much more! I've not properly called you by name. Thank you for being all this to me. I will remember it more often when I call on *YOUR NAME!*

"I, Jesus, have sent my angel to give you this
testimony for the churches. I am the Root
and the Offspring of David, and the bright
Morning Star."
—Revelation 22:16 NIV

"But one of the elders said to me,
'Do not weep. Behold, the Lion of the tribe of
Judah, the Root of David, has prevailed to open
the scroll and to loose its seven seals.'"
—Revelation 5:5 NKJV

"Moses built an altar there and named it
Yahweh-Nissi (which means
'the Lord is my banner.')"
—Exodus 17:15 NLT

THE PEANUT GALLERY

Hi God. Could you tell these knuckleheads in the peanut gallery to pipe down? Everybody seems to want to weigh in on what I have going on. And most of them have never even thought about trying to do what I'm doing!

What's the deal? Everybody's an instant expert just because they can run Google? I get it, that information is out there. But I don't need information. I don't need statistics. I don't need to see what Google, Alexa, Siri, or anybody else says – unless it's YOU!

When I say that I'm going to pray about it, it seems like everything moves so slow that I need a calendar instead of a stopwatch. I know people like to move fast. It's obvious that people try to talk like they know what's up. But when it comes down to brass tacks, unless they've done what I want to do . . . they aren't really the people I need to talk to about this.

AND (that's a capital A-N-D), if they aren't willing to pray with me and see what you have to say about it – well, they might not be the kind of person I want in my think tank. Man's plans versus God's ways. If they don't pray, they don't stay on the advisory board of my life!

There is one "chief seat" on this committee, and it belongs to you! After that, I'm co-chair of my life. And the rest of the seats at the table? They need to be filled with people who've actually done the things that I feel that you're beckoning my heart to do.

I need someone who can point out the pitfalls. Counsel me around the carnage. Comrades to help spring the traps. People WAY more successful than me, so they don't mind when I succeed, too!

Pride will make people talk. Pride will also take me down. A fool loves the sound of his own voice. Lord, deliver from the *"peanut gallery,"* and send me Heavenly advisors that have YOU as their cornerstone of wisdom!

God's Word

"Where there is no guidance, a people falls,
but in an abundance of counselors, there is safety."
—Proverbs 11:14 ESV

"Blessed is the man who walks not in the counsel
of the ungodly, nor stands in the path of sinners,
nor sits in the seat of the scornful; but his delight
is in the law of the Lord, and in His law he meditates
day and night. He shall be like a tree planted
by the rivers of water, that brings forth its fruit
in its season, whose leaf also shall not wither;
and whatever he does shall prosper. The ungodly
are not so, but are like the chaff which the wind
drives away. Therefore the ungodly shall not stand
in the judgment, nor sinners in the congregation
of the righteous. For the Lord knows the way of the
righteous, but the way of the ungodly shall perish."
—Psalm 1:1-6 NKJV

LONG TIME NO SEE

Hi God. It seems like it's been too long between visits. Not like, *"Hi. I love you. Could you? I need you! Thank you! Amen,"* But a REAL talk!

It's not that I don't want to. I DO . . . more than you know! I need to be with you. It . . .settles me. Being with you breathes life into me. It fills me up. It lets me know that I don't have to have it all together, because you do—and you're on the case for me!

And yet, bills, phones, texts, laundry, work, just this one last email, kids, tiredness, running late . . . Oops! I didn't plan on that! LIFE HAPPENS!

And with all of the stolen seconds and minutes adding up, somehow, they subtract from the time I was planning on spending with you!

Maybe that's because you are the ONE person, thing, situation, that's NOT going to scream for my attention. You sit back and W-A-I-T, oh so patiently, for me to realize that I am spinning like the rainbow wheel on my computer. It goes round and round, and never seems to get anything done!

You're a gentleman in a world full of lights, sounds, alerts, badges, buzzers, alarms, and reminders. The way you tug on my heart is so soft and gentle . . . and so easy to push to the back of the line.

Why is it that, what I need MOST is what I seem to reach for LAST?

Nothing else has worked? Well then, I'll pray about it. The enemy has really got a strong distraction game happening. He's trying to keep me from the ONE thing that gives me power, victory, courage, strength, blessing, peace – 'the edge.' You! You are what makes me sharp and able.

Lord, help me to tune out the nonsense that 'needs' me and turn to what I need. I NEED YOU!

And when I unplug from the overwhelming buzz of the world and prioritize you as the maker of the universe and the giver of peace, you harmonize the craziness of life into a symphony of opportunity.

Your wisdom guides me. Your knowledge is supreme! Your peace flows like a river. Your love gives me the ability to have forgiveness and compassion. When I make time for you, you transform me from a shell of a person who walks around fragile and easily broken. You fortify me into the fearless and faith-filled person you created me to be!

World, you're going to have to wait your turn. Talk to the hand—the face ain't listenin'.

Neither is my heart.

Thank you for not giving up on me! I'm late to the party, but you won't hold that against me. You're the kind of Father who puts a ring on my finger and a robe on my back, even when I don't deserve it.

I have so much to talk to you about . . .

"For this is what the LORD says: 'I will extend peace to her like a river, and the wealth of nations like a flooding stream; you will nurse and be carried on her arm and dandled on her knees.'"
—Isaiah 66:12 NIV

"And we, who with unveiled faces all reflect the Lord's glory, are being transformed into his likeness with ever-increasing glory, which comes from the Lord, who is the Spirit."
—2 Corinthians 3:18 NIV

"So he got up and went to his father. But while he was still a long way off, his father saw him and was filled with compassion for him; he ran to his son, threw his arms around him and kissed him. The son said to him, 'Father, I have sinned against heaven and against you. I am no longer worthy to be called your son.' But the father said to his servants, 'Quick! Bring the best robe and put it on him. Put a ring on his finger and sandals on his feet.'"
—Luke 15:20-22 NIV

JOY JEALOUS

Hi God. When I walk through a store and people are strolling down the aisle humming and singing, it gets on my nerves! Is it because they're happy and I wish I was? Am I seriously irritated because they're joyful? Am I *joy jealous?*

Well, if I'm jealous for the *fruit of the Spirit* that they have, how do I get that?

The Bible says that, as I trust YOU (not me), YOU (not my job), YOU (not them to do the right thing), YOU (not me working harder) . . . as I trust YOU, joy and peace come.

If I don't have joy and peace—which obviously right now is a problem (hence, the irritation with the happy people)—it's a TRUST problem. Why don't I trust you? That's crazy! You can handle anything!

I must need to talk to you more. When I'm with you, when I'm in your presence, I'm happy. It's when I forget our morning meetings that my attitude starts heading to *Grinchville*. Okay, let's be honest – sometimes, by afternoon, I need a joy REFRESH!

When I'm in your presence, I'm reminded of your promises. When I read your Word, I'm reminded of your promises. When I pray, I'm reminded of your promises. When I reside in your promises and not my problems, things shift in my head and in my heart.

That's probably why you tell me to pray without ceasing. I need a constant joy infusion! I don't need to "joy" once. I need to *RE-joy-CE* over and over again.

I can do this! I can trust you with the problem, lean into the promise, and get my mouth moving about things I am thankful for instead of things I wish would change. Like that lady singing. Wait . . . I think I know that song!

A simple shift in my heart because of a few minutes with you, and I can feel things changing in my heart and mind. I'm going to keep talking to you. When I'm thankful, it makes my heart full . . . and now I'm joyful!

Wait a minute! Maybe, I AM full of it . . . JOY! Now, I'm laughing, and people are looking at me weird. Suddenly, I'm the annoying happy person! Thanks, God!

God's Word

"May the God of hope fill you with all joy
and peace as you trust in him, so that you may
overflow with hope by the power of the Holy Spirit."
—Romans 15:13 NIV

"You make known to me the path of life;
in your presence there is fullness of joy;
at your right hand are pleasures forevermore."
—Psalm 16:11 ESV

"Rejoice always, pray without ceasing,
give thanks in all circumstances; for this is the will
of God in Christ Jesus for you."
—1 Thessalonians 5:16-18 ESV

WHY DO I SEE
AND SAY?

Hi God. I remember a toy for little kids. You pull the string, (or, nowadays, kids push the handle) and it would spin around and around until it landed on a picture. Wherever it stopped, it said what the picture was. I think they're called a "See and Say."

Even a machine with no brain can say what it sees. That doesn't take a lot of faith, wisdom, or trust. But it seems like I act just like a *human* See and Say sometimes. I see with my natural eyes what's happening around me, and my mouth just *goes to town*. "I can't believe . . ." "I feel so . . ." "It just hurts . . ." and on and on.

It's like I think I get a *free pass* just because I'm "just being real." However, you didn't ask me to be real. You didn't command me to live by what I see—to spray that everywhere with the power of my mouth.

Instead, you said to *walk by faith*. You said to *live by faith*. You want my faith in your miracle-working power to be so much stronger than what's sitting right in front of me—even if it's the size of a mountain:

A mountain of debt; a mountain of laundry; a mountain of emotions I haven't been able to deal with;

mountainous anxiety; a mountain-sized "to-do" list and no time to do; a mountain of hurt?

Mountains don't scare you, God; and so they aren't supposed to scare me . . .not when you're here with me.

You don't want me to give a detailed description of the mountain. Why do I do that, anyway? To get others to feel bad for me? To impress people with all the things I'm dealing with? Impressing them isn't going to help. And getting their mouths to agree with mine is the opposite of what I need!

You tell me to look that mountain squarely in the eye, stand firm in faith, and don't give it one tiny word of acknowledgment. Instead, I need to tell that mountain *who* my Father is, *how much* my Father loves me, *what* the Bible says about the promises my Father has given me, and *command it* to take a flying leap into the ocean! That way, I never have to see it again, and neither does anyone else!

If the mountain tries to stay . . .I'll just walk away, like Jesus did from the fig tree He cursed. The tree didn't die within minutes, but it began the process immediately. His disciples couldn't see the proof with their eyes yet. But it was dying on the inside.

That's why there should be a big difference between what we *see* and what we *say*. Sometimes, I see so little of what you're actually doing for me behind the scenes. I'm not going to say what I see in the natural. I'm going to say what you, God, have *promised* to do for me!

"So may the words of my mouth,
my meditation-thoughts, and every movement of my
heart be always pure and pleasing, acceptable before
your eyes, my only Redeemer, my Protector-God."
—Psalm 19:14 TPT

"I tell you the truth, you can say to this mountain,
'May you be lifted up and thrown into the sea,'
and it will happen. But you must really believe it will
happen and have no doubt in your heart. I tell you,
you can pray for anything, and if you believe that
you've received it, it will be yours."
—Mark 11:23-24 NLT

"I pray that the eyes of your heart may be
enlightened in order that you may know the hope
to which he has called you, the riches of his glorious
inheritance in his holy people."
—Ephesians 1:18 NIV

WHY ARE THEY
SO MEAN?

Hi God. I think I'm a nice person. I mean, I *try.* Sometimes, it seems like other people don't even try to be nice.

I mean, seriously! Why would people be so nasty to complete strangers on social media? Why do people at work act nice to my face, and then talk about me behind my back? How is it that my neighbors can be so sweet in front of me and so sassy when I'm not around? Really? Even my family sometimes says, "That's too big for somebody like you."

These jabs and attacks make me want to quit.

I know that you don't want me to let my haters keep me from dreaming. You don't want criticism to make me freeze like somebody doing the mannequin challenge. You don't want me to slow down. You've always known that there's an enemy out there and he has a big mouth.

Haters gonna hate!

That's what they do. How hater acts and what I do shouldn't look the same at all. They chatter like birds in the background. They bark like dogs when a stranger walks by. Barking dogs don't have anything to do with me! After all, I *am* a stranger to them. I'm positive. I'm a believer. I'm a dreamer! I certainly won't let those haters keep me from dreaming.

Any nameless fool can hide behind a fake alias on social media and type slurs at other people. I can either allow that fool to determine my future, or I can lean on the God of heaven and earth. Honestly, that's not a tough choice. I'm going with you! You're already ahead of whatever hate, hurt, hell, or hurdle will get in my way, next.

Nothing takes you by surprise. You created the end from the beginning. You saw these haters coming decades before they were even born. You manufactured a way of escape for me, and figured out how to turn their hate and harassment into a way for me to get ahead!

Whatever the enemy slings, you turn around and use for my promotion. Whatever the haters spout, you repurpose for my blessing.

If I can trust in you . . . I'll do it. You're faithful. You're true. You've never left me. I'm not going to let these pups and parakeets steal my future. I've got the God of the universe on my side!

God's Word

"Be alert and of sober mind. Your enemy the devil
prowls around like a roaring lion looking
for someone to devour."
—1 Peter 5:8 NIV

"You will be hated by all because of my life
in you. But don't worry. My grace will never desert
you or depart from your life. And by standing
firm with patient endurance you will find
your souls' deliverance."
—Luke 21:17-19 TPT

"But blessed are those who trust in the
LORD and have made the LORD their hope
and confidence."
—Jeremiah 17:7 NLT

PEEK-A-BOO

Hi God. Seven . . .eight . . .nine . . .ten. Ok, time's up! Where are you? . . .Where am I?

Sometimes, I feel like I'm playing hide-and-go-seek with you.

I can't see you and I feel like I can't find you. Are you around the corner? Upstairs? Are you watching me look for you? Am I hot or cold? I wonder if you can see me.

And then . . .*peek-a-boo*! I get a glimpse of you—in a feeling in my heart, in prayer, in worship, or in something that happens to me. And when I feel that I can't see you anymore . . . I want to even more!

Why is it that I identify—more than I want to—with a two-year-old playing peek-a-boo? Anxious, a little confused, but still so eagerly anticipating that next glimpse of the person they love. And then so overwhelmed with glee when they finally find them! That's me looking for you. I still can't help wondering if you see me.

This peek-a-boo reminds me of when life got so hard for Hagar that she ran away into the wilderness. Even though no one knew where to find her, you did. You knew where she was. You knew *how* she was. You saw her. You never stop. You never leave. You never look away. You can *always* see me, no matter how alone I might feel.

Now, you want me to look at you. Regardless if my own hands and actions are in the way of me seeing you (peek-a-boo style), or if there are other hurdles, you want me to look at you. Whether I'm trying to run away from my problems, like Hagar was, or standing still, looking at the complications and then trying to catch a glimpse of you around them.

I might not be able to see you . . .but you're there. You want me to be confident even when I can't get a glimpse of you. You're still working. Maybe I can't see you. But that doesn't mean anything is wrong. That simply means it's time for my faith to activate.

As long as I know you can see me, I can fix my eyes on what I can't see. You are here. Your grace surrounds me. Your love envelopes me. Your mercy engulfs me. It's time! No more hide-and-seek. No more peek-a-boo. I'm not looking for you, God. I'm looking right at you and your goodness. I'll keep my eye on the ball. I won't get distracted.

You are with me. You see me. And now, I commit to looking right back at you. Together, we can do anything!

God's Word

"Then she called the name of the Lord who spoke to her, 'You are God Who Sees'; for she said, 'Have I not even here [in the wilderness] remained alive after seeing Him [who sees me with understanding and compassion]?' Therefore the well was called Beer-lahai-roi (Well of the Living One Who Sees Me); it is between Kadesh and Bered."
—Genesis 16:13-14 AMP

"So we fix our eyes not on what is seen, but on what is unseen, since what is seen is temporary, but what is unseen is eternal."
—2 Corinthians 4:18 NIV

"Then Jesus told him, 'You believe because you have seen me. Blessed are those who believe without seeing me.'"
—John 20:29 NLT

I HIT THE WALL

Hi God. It happened: I was running and gunning. I was going and blowing. I was pushing through. I was telling myself, *"You can do this!"* And I was! I was doing it . . . until now.

I just got *tired* . . . I thought I had this. I'm so disappointed. I keep trying to get up, but I just can't seem to muster the strength. I'm so mad at myself for stopping. If only I had . . . *what?* Never sat down? Never quit?

Keep moving. Go through the motions. It all feels so robotic, but at least things were happening. What's the problem? Why didn't it work? It did for a little while. Maybe I was relying on my own strength. I was pushing me, but not praying to you.

What I can do by myself and what I can do when I lean into you are two different things. I have no idea why I forget that. You aren't human. You don't get tired. You never sleep. You're the charge that will recharge me—*if* I'll plug into you.

What was I thinking? I remember to plug my phone in, but forget to connect to you, my power source. With you, all things are possible! With you, I can exceed my own expectations and begin to live up to yours! With you, there is access to heaven, time, healing, provision, favor, opportunity, and supernatural guidance. With you, I can avoid all the "time-wasters" and have heavenly insight on where to invest my energy for maximum return.

No more hamster wheel runs for me! I'm not doing what I want, but what you LEAD me to do, even if I feel unsure. This way I'll call all the right people at all the perfect times. I'll be sending all the immaculately-worded emails to the exact people they need to go to and reaping phenomenal results! That's how it works when I'm led by you and not me.

My time and effort are being maximized beyond what I could ever do with 110% effort 24 hours a day. Why? Because the *King of All Time and Wisdom* is my business partner, leading, guiding, and directing every move I make with supernatural influence!

I won't extend my leg for *one more step* without you directing my decisions! Wall? Hit *what* wall? There is no wall that cannot be broken through, no mountain that is not forced to move, and no enemy that can withstand the power of *my* God!

I'm ready to go with you, Jesus!

God's Word

"Indeed, he who watches over Israel never
slumbers or sleeps."
—Psalm 121:4 NLT

"It is God who arms me with strength,
and makes my way perfect."
—Psalm 18:32 NKJV

"But Jesus looked at them and said to them,
'With men this is impossible, but with God
all things are possible.'"
—Matthew 19:26 NKJV

RUNNING ON EMPTY

Hi God. You're not as loud and pesky as everyone else is . . .

Send the email!
Hurry up!
We need that report!
I'm hungry!
Where are you? You're LATE!

Everyone else doesn't mind voicing their needs and complaining until I fill them. Everyone else wants me to pour out; but I feel like I'm running on empty. Yet, I know if I can just get close to you, I can breathe . . . you will fill me up!

It seems like life doesn't allow for "luxuries" like breathing . . . and Jesus. I need to breathe. I need you. But *how* do I get time with you?

Fill me up, Lord—but do it in the express lane, as I speed by, a few miles over the speed limit. Oh, and P.S.: Please have the police look the other way . . . just for today.

You won't be bossy, rude, or demanding. You'll wait quietly, in the background, for me to come to you—watching, wishing I would realize that you are my answer.

I guess, once I run out of steam, I'll have no other options but you. *Or*, I could realize in this very moment that, even though I can't possibly afford to stop, I really can't afford *not* to stop and meet with you . . . the most important meeting of my day.

When we talk, you tell me who is going to waste my time, what isn't worth the hassle, and what game-changers to my future I'm about to overlook. You give me strength to handle the conversations I would have messed up without you. You give me the patience not to "cut off my nose to spite my face." You give me wisdom so that words, wiser than my years and experience, flow out when I speak.

You make me *so much more* than I am!

If I could just see that these few minutes I don't realize I have are actually the most important moments of my day . . .They're the saving grace that'll save me from the trouble I can't even see—my fuel—my refill—my *everything*!

How did I possibly think I had no time to have you pour into me? You pour in kindness, wisdom, strength, courage, confidence, grace, blessing, and the ability to bless others.

Father, forgive me for losing sight of what's truly important. You are my priority. Silly me—I hadn't paused long enough to see that I've *always* needed you!

God's Word

"He strengthens those who are weak and tired.
Even those who are young grow weak; young people
can fall exhausted. But those who trust in the LORD
for help will find their strength renewed. They will rise
on wings like eagles; they will run and not get weary;
they will walk and not grow weak."
—Isaiah 40:29-31 GNT

"Seek the Kingdom of God above all else,
and live righteously, and he will give you everything
you need. So don't worry about tomorrow,
for tomorrow will bring its own worries.
Today's trouble is enough for today."
—Matthew 6:33-34 NLT

"Don't worry about anything; instead,
pray about everything. Tell God what you need,
and thank him for all he has done. Then you will
experience God's peace, which exceeds anything
we can understand. His peace will guard your hearts
and minds as you live in Christ Jesus."
—Philippians 4:6-7 NLT

I NEED TO MAKE A DECISION

Hi God. I *seriously* need to figure this out.

I don't know what to do. But if I do nothing . . . that's still doing something. I don't want to make a decision to do *nothing*. Come on! I need to know what to do!

"Do I stay or do I go?" isn't just a line from a song. It's the reality of where I'm stuck. I'm looking both ways. I can't afford to screw this up!

I know I make a million decisions every day without checking in with you. Some of them are easy because "Ain't NO WAY I'm doing *that*—hello!" Emotional decisions are easy. Except, I've lived to regret a lot of those. Actually, the thing I *don't* want to do, in the moment, is usually the right thing.

I guess emotions aren't the way I should guide my decisions. But I use emotions to make like ten to twenty decisions a day. Wait! How many decisions do I make every day without asking you, God???

I need a new decision-making plan. When I need to know something, I'm not going to go with what I know. I see where that's gotten me. I'm going to lean into you. I'll pause, pray, listen for peace, and obey. That's a formula for good decisions.

It doesn't take but a second to pause and ask you what to do. Why wouldn't I ask the One who knows every possible outcome? Every word you say drips with the wisdom of the ages.

The Bible says you lead me with peace. So I'll check with you. It's not that you're not leading. I just haven't been checking the right indicators. Okay, I might have overridden a couple of them, because my sense of peace didn't line up with what I wanted.

I won't simply go with what I THINK I want in the moment, anymore. Instead, I'll lean into my spirit and see what YOU say. I'm listening for that heavenly peace.

And when I have peace in a direction, I won't ignore it. I won't override it. I'll obey it. With you, God, it's never for less . . . it's always for more! The willing and obedient (that's me) eat the good of the land (Isaiah 1:19). Now, it's time to feast on some good decisions!

God's Word

"If you are willing and obedient, you will eat
the good things of the land."
—Isaiah 1:19 NIV

"Trust in the Lord with all of your heart,
and do not lean on your own understanding.
In all your ways acknowledge him, and he will
make your paths straight."
—Proverbs 3:5-6 ESV

"For the Lord gives wisdom; from his mouth comes
knowledge and understanding."
—Proverbs 2:6 NIV

"Let the peace of Christ [the inner calm of one who
walks daily with Him] be the controlling factor in your
hearts [deciding and settling questions that arise].
To this *peace* indeed you were called as members
in one body [of believers]. And be thankful
[to God always]."
—Colossians 3:15 AMP

BROKEN

Hi God. I look around on social media, and everybody's life looks so . . .*FUN!* Then, there's me. Less "likes" and sometimes I feel as if no one cares. Why am I the only one with a hole in my timeline? Why do their stories seem great when my life seems broken?

The enemy does his best to hide the fact that *everybody* has experienced brokenness. He wants me to feel like an outcast—alone, singled out, and like I can't keep up with everyone. But everybody has had times when they've been financially "broke," a relationship has "broken up." Many of us came from, or are afraid that we could be headed towards, a "broken home."

Our hearts have been broken; our bodies have broken, whether it's a bone, a tumor, or an illness; our past is so messed up that our future seems broken. At least, that's what the enemy whispers to us.

Not true. God, you tell me the same thing two different places in the Bible: You came to heal the *broken*. You came because of my broken places—you came to fill the void! You knew this current situation was coming my way, and you've already planned a way of escape; a healing inside of me; a way to use what the enemy meant for evil . . . for my good!

If the enemy is going to bother "your baby," you're going to make him pay! Instead of calling me a lost cause, you let your light shine through my broken places to show the world what your light can do if I will let you. And I want to let you do just that! There is purpose in my pain, and I will use it for your gain!

It's the most remarkable thing: the place where a bone has been broken heals stronger than it was before the break—and the bone won't break in the same place again! You are healing me stronger than I was before, so that I won't break THERE again. I might have *been* broken; but THIS is never happening to me again!

The enemy tried to break me down; but when I'm weak, you are strong. And I'm stronger than ever in you when I allow you to heal me!

It didn't kill me. *I . . .AM . . .STILL . . .HERE!* God, I might have broken places right now; but I invite you in to heal, repair, replace, renew, revitalize, restore, and make me stronger than ever. Use my restoration story for your glory!

God's Word

"The Spirit of the Lord GOD *is* upon Me,
because the LORD has anointed Me to preach
good tidings to the poor; He has sent Me to heal the
brokenhearted, to proclaim liberty to the captives,
and the opening of the prison to *those who are* bound."
—Isaiah 61:1 NKJV

*"'The Spirit of the LORD is upon Me, because He has
anointed Me to preach the gospel to the poor; He has sent Me
to heal the brokenhearted, to proclaim liberty to the captives
and recovery of sight to the blind, to set at liberty those who are
oppressed; to proclaim the acceptable year of the LORD.'* Then
He closed the book, and gave *it* back to
the attendant and sat down. And the eyes of all
who were in the synagogue were fixed on Him.
And He began to say to them, 'Today this Scripture
is fulfilled in your hearing.'"
—Luke 4:18-21 NKJV

The Lord is close to the brokenhearted and saves
those who are crushed in spirit.
—Psalm 34:18 NIV

I'M READY FOR
THE RIDE

Hi God. I feel like I need to put on my safety belt and keep all arms and legs inside the cabin at all times. It just feels like I'm on a *rockin' rollercoaster* ready to take off!

When something new and exciting is about to happen, it can make me nervous. My palms sweat, my stomach feels a little funny—and it has nothing to do with last night's dinner. I'm excited . . . but almost terrified all in the same moment.

If I wasn't already strapped in, I might jump off right now. I don't care what people think! But I don't want to miss the ride either.

You have CRAZY plans for me. They feel like the beginning of a wild ride! I'm intimidated, but my job isn't the hard one.

All I have to do is HOLD ON! I don't need to try to drive the train; instead, I can let you take me to the place I need to go. Even if it takes me upside down and sideways for a minute . . .with you at the helm, I know I'm safe. I'm not just safe; I'm completely psyched and screaming my head off in excitement!

I would never try any of this on my own. But I'm not alone. I'm with you! When I get nervous, and the hills seem crazy steep, and I know the drop afterward is something to be reckoned with – I can look over at you and know this: as I look to you and trust, you will never lead me astray!

The ride might feel crazy, but the destination you are taking me to a good place: a green, luscious pasture full of provision, nutrition, and capacity. The road may be wild, but it leads to a place of still water where I am sustained, given peace, and washed of all those things I've been carrying.

You don't do any of this for me because I deserve it. You do it because you're my Father. And if I follow your instructions, even when it scares me a little, you'll lead me on the ride of my life! I'll be jumping up and down and shouting, *"Do it again, Daddy! Can we do it again?"*

Even though this ride I'm on right now looks scarier than the last one, you're right beside me. You're comforting me, encouraging me, telling me I can do it if I trust you. And I do!

Okay, let's do this thing!

God's Word

"Behold, I am doing a new thing; now it springs forth, do you not perceive it? I will make a way in the wilderness and rivers in the desert."
—Isaiah 43:19 ESV

"The Lord *is* my shepherd; I shall not want. He makes me to lie down in green pastures; He leads me beside the still waters."
—Psalm 23:1-2 NKJV

"Yea, though I walk through the valley of the shadow of death, I will fear no evil; For You *are* with me; Your rod and Your staff, they comfort me."
—Psalm 23:4 NKJV